PARADISE LOST

Crested Crane
Uganda's National Symbol

PARADISE LOST:

A History of Game Preservation in

EAST AFRICA

Thomas P. Ofcansky

West Virginia UniversityPress
Morgantown
2002

West Virginia University Press, Morgantown 26506
Copyright© 2002 by West Virginia University Press
All rights reserved
First edition 2002
Printed in the United States of America
10 09 08 07 06 05 04 03 02   5 4 3 2 1

ISBN 0-937058-61-0

Library of Congress Cataloging-in-Publication Data

Ofcansky, Thomas P. 1947-
Paradise Lost: A History of Game Preservation in East Africa
160 p illus. map 26 cm
Includes bibliographical references and index.

1. Africa, East — History.
2. Game preservation —Africa, East.
3. Game reserves—Africa, East—History
I. Title.   2001012345
                          CIP

Cover Photograph courtesy of Thomas P. Ofcansky
Edited by John Luchok
Book design by Angela Caudill , West Virginia University Publications Services
Printed in USA

Surely it is obvious enough, if one looks at the whole world that it is becoming daily better cultivated and more fully peopled. All places are now accessible, all are well known; most pleasant farms have obliterated all traces of what were once dreary and dangerous wastes; cultivated fields and subdued forests, flocks and herds have expelled wild beasts; sandy deserts are sown, rocks are planted; marshes are drained; and where once were hardly solitary cottages, there are now large cities.

—Tertullian 337 A.D.

Contents

Illustrations

Foreword

Many people have described, though few can now remember, the sight that met the eyes of early twentieth-century travellers on the old Uganda Railway when they rolled up the blinds of their carriages at dawn to take their first look at the East African highlands. Away to the west arose the great bulk of Mount Kilimanjaro, like a table spread with a white cloth, and in the foreground—that is, if the season was right—grazed and moved tens of thousands of wild animals of every species from massive rhinos to the beautiful dappled giraffe. Although you seldom saw elephants, but you might, there were many kinds of antelope and gazelle, and, if your eyes were keen enough, you might see a scuttling mongoose or a little bat-eared fox. This was one of the sights of the world, and everyone who bought a ticket from Mombasa to Nairobi could enjoy it at certain times of the year. It was by no means unique. All over East Africa, in forest, bushland and plain, wild animals abounded. What scientists call the biomass—the total weight of living creatures in a given area—was probably unequalled, and so too the variety; about 380 species of mammals, let alone birds and reptiles, have been recorded in the East African terrain.

In this now vanished world, the animals seemed inexhaustible, as much a permanent part of the landscape as rivers or trees. It occurred to very few of us that in our lifetimes the animals, like forests that are felled and rivers that run dry, would dwindle to a shadow of their former abundance and, over most of these seemingly limitless highlands, simply disappear.

People, of course, were also present, but in very small numbers. Many were nomadic, seeking with their flocks and herds the fresh grass that sprang up after rain, and moving with their few possessions from one cluster of temporary dwellings to the next. Gradually, the cultivating tribes cleared tongues of forest and shifted with their crops into well-watered and more favorable regions. Equipped only with bows and poisoned arrows, spears and traps, these tribesmen protected their crops and livestock as best they could from tramplers and predators; but, with few exceptions, did not slay the animals for meat. Now and again an animal retaliated by pouncing on a human, but, by and large, a state of coexistence between man and wild animal was maintained. Elephants were an exception. Ivory had been prized by man since biblical times and beyond, and long before the colonial era, Arab caravans bearing tusks and driving yoked slaves—the two trades went well together, the stronger slaves carrying the tusks—had been trudging down to the coast. The elephant population had sustained these losses without apparent damage; and, of course, some of the loot was "recovered" ivory taken from elephants that had died a natural death.

The "opening up" of Africa following the colonial "scramble" changed all this. The first and most obvious consequence, though not the most significant, was the appearance of the high-velocity rifle in the hands of sportsmen intent on killing as many creatures as they could. Animals were slaughtered in great numbers—as a single example, a captain in the Indian Army on safari near Mount Kilimanjaro shot sixty-six rhinos in a few days—and, in South Africa, by the end of the nineteenth century, the blaabok and the quagga had already become extinct.

In Britain some authorities, including scientists and men of the then ruling class, read the writing on the wall. As early as 1897, Britain's Foreign Office, which then controlled the newly constituted British East Africa Protectorate, promulgated a game preservation ordinance which established a sanctuary for the wildlife and regulated hunting by means of licenses. Delegates to an international conference held in London signed a convention in 1900 "for the Preservation of Animals, Birds and Fish in Africa." Three years later, the Society for the Preservation of the Wild Fauna of the Empire was started, which, renamed the Fauna Preservation Society, is still very much in business today. That was the start of the movement to guard from extinction those that remained of the great concourse of wild creatures, a story which Dr. Thomas P. Ofcansky has movingly told in the following pages.

It was not, of course, the start of game preservation in the world at large. The world's first National Park, the Yellowstone, took shape in the United States in 1872. Long before that, kings and emperors had preserved for sport or for scientific interest species considered, even then, to be endangered by man's rapacity, indifference or greed. The Inca kings, for example, protected the vicuna, which was rounded up and shorn at intervals but never killed; its fine, silk-like fleece was woven into royal garments by virgins of the Temple of the Sun. The Mogul emperor Mohammed Akbar set aside reserves so large that more than 5,000 elephants were said to have found sanctuary therein.

It was not until our present century that the real threat to the survival of the animals arose. We all know by now whence that threat has come: from the human womb. There are plenty of statistics to prove what we can easily see for ourselves: that the human species is multiplying with almost bacterial speed. For the many thousand years that Homo Sapiens has walked the earth, the rate of increase was gradual, until, in the last century, the world's population started its spectacular increase. This gathered momentum slowly at first, until, in the middle of our present century came the explosion. Between 1940 and 1980, human population more than doubled. Barring some disaster such as nuclear war, the rise will continue at an exponential rate, like compound interest, and nothing will stop it from passing the six thousand million mark by the year 2000. More than half the population of many countries is under eighteen years of age.

Kenya is one such country and it has one of the highest birthrates in the world. When I first arrived there, in 1913, the population guesstimate was two and a half million. Today the figure is over seventeen million. The great majority, despite the growth of towns, are peasant farmers needing land to cultivate and on which to run their livestock, as well as timber for firewood and building, charcoal for fuel, and water for survival. The human tide sweeps over forest, bush and plain. Everywhere the wild animals must literally give ground. As the zoologist Dr. Richard Laws has written, "the distribution of man and elephant populations has changed from one characterized by human islands in a sea of elephants, to increasingly small islands of elephants in a sea of people."

Dr. Ofcansky traces the stages by which a policy of preserving the animals themselves developed into one of setting aside for them certain habitats. Kenya led the way by gazetting the first National Park in 1947. This was the tiny Nairobi Park, only 44 miles in extent, but astonishingly rich in its variety of species. In all three territories, other parks followed. The colonial governments aimed at securing the independence of their parks by putting them under the management of boards of trustees. From the start, National Parks were money-spinners for the governments concerned. Tourism has become one of Kenya's and Tanzania's major industries and earners of foreign exchange (Uganda, in 1990, still is recovering from the collapse of law and order and the troubled situation that followed). For this reason, if for no other, tourism is supported and encouraged by the East African governments, which in the last twenty years have not only greatly improved the tourists' amenities but provided better training and equipment for the wardens and rangers who look after the parks.

So, in theory, the parks should be secure and the animals within them safe from harassment. As with so many human affairs, theory is one thing and practice another. There is, for instance, the question of poaching. As trophies—horns, tusks, pelts, and so on—grow scarcer, prices rise and the rewards of poaching escalate; so, also, do the poachers' equipment and techniques grow more sophisticated and harder to counter. The black rhino in particular, with its much sought after horn, has been poached to the brink of extinction over most of its former range. Then, paradoxically, the larger mammals, boxed into their sanctuaries by the certainty of slaughter if they venture out, are, in certain cases, multiplying to a point where they are seriously damaging, and even destroying, their habitat. Migration routes which formerly enabled them to trek away from areas whose food supply they had exhausted to fresh pastures—a form of crop rotation—have been closed to them by human settlements.

This human pressure on the land must inevitably escalate as the population grows. Considerable areas of the Maasai country in Kenya, for example, have been ploughed for wheat production. These are not inside the Maasai-Mara National Park but near its perimeter, thus further confining the animals within the park. Range management projects are also depriving the animals of the freedom of movement they need. Maasai pastoralists resent the exclusion of their cattle from that part of their former range that lies within the Serengeti National Park in Tanzania. The pressure mounts. A simple legislative measure brought the National Parks into existence; an equally simple measure could snuff them out.

World opinion, however, is now firmly on the side of National Parks. An international outcry could be expected to greet any measure intended to weaken or even abolish them. The International Union for the Conservation of Nature and Natural Resources (I.U.C.N.), centered near Geneva, is a watchdog guarding the parks' integrity and urging governments—for it has no power of its own—to resist temptations to treat their parks as regions for development rather than as sanctuaries for wildlife. (There have been schemes to build dams and reservoirs, to exercise land for farming, to conduct logging operations in National Parks, even one to build a railway across the Serengeti, which conservationists have resisted with a considerable measure, so far, of success.) In the last resort, world-wide public opinion will determine the safety, or spoilation, of the parks. Whether this opinion can be mobilized in sufficient strength to defend the wildlife sanctuaries against the growing needs of hungry humans is a question that must be answered in the next fifty years.

Dr. Ofcansky has taken a close, informed and realistic look at the situation as it obtains today and his conclusion is not optimistic. "Man and animal," he concludes, "cannot live together side by side in peace and harmony. The only realistic wildlife preservation policy is therefore one that would delay rather than prevent the destruction of East Africa's fauna."

Yet we should not despair. Given protection, plants and animals show remarkable resilience in recovering from onslaughts of man and climate alike. Through tourism, the parks constitute an asset which no African country could afford to do without. If mankind has the will to save them, the parks and denizens can survive. Dr. Ofcansky's study is a valuable contribution to the literature of conservation and wildlife management and I am honored to introduce it to, I hope, a wide circle of readers. To all of us his topic is important, and to the wild animals literally a matter of life or death.

—*Elspeth Huxley (1907-1997)*

Acknowledgments

This book began as a doctoral dissertation while the writer was a doctoral student at West Virginia University. My thanks are extended to West Virginia University's Department of History, especially to Dr. Robert M. Maxon, and to Dr. W.R. McLeod. The late Don Bond of the Perley Isaac Reed School of Journalism read and reread endless drafts of the manuscript. A debt of gratitude is owed to the late Dr. Robert F. Munn, Dean of the West Virginia University Libraries and editor of the West Virginia University Press, who assisted in the revision of the manuscript. His untimely death was a loss to the University and to the academic community at large. His successor, Dr. Ruth M. Jackson, guided the manuscript through its initial production process and Dr. Patrick Conner ensured its publication. John Luchok, Director of Publication Services, made numerous helpful editorial suggestions. Lastly, Dr. Roger Yeager of the Department of Political Science provided sound advice and invaluable assistance which helped the manuscript through the final editorial process.

In conducting research, the writer was fortunate to have the assistance of many institutions, not limited to but including the Public Record Office (PRO); the Royal Commonwealth Society whose collection is now housed in the Cambridge University Library; the Institute of Commonwealth Studies; the School of Oriental and African Studies; and the Museum of Natural History Library, Reference Division—all of which are in the United Kingdom—were most generous with their time and advice. Equally helpful were the library staff at the University of Nairobi and at the McMillan Memorial Library in Kenya. In the United States, the libraries at Syracuse University, Michigan State University, and West Virginia University provided much invaluable material.

The individuals who read the manuscript or answered my numerous questions about colonial East Africa are too numerous to mention. I offer special thanks to the late George Adamson, the late Rennie Bere, the late Leda Farrant, Ian Grimwood, the late Hugh Lamprey, Sir Francis Loyd, the late A.T. Matson, the late John Owen, Noel Simon, John Webster, and John Burton. I also would like to thank the late Elspeth Huxley who wrote the foreword in 1990. Although much has happened to East Africa's wildlife since then, her observation and judgements remain valid. No changes have been made to her foreword. The manuscript also benefitted from the assistance of numerous other individuals, including Kraig Adler, Monty Brown,

A.M.H. Henley, Pascal James Imperato, Margaret D. Kummerfeldt, David McCabe, and Gerald Rilling.

My appreciation for the support and encouragement I received from family and friends, especially E.E. and S.B., cannot be expressed adequately. Hopefully, publication of this book will be of some recompense to them.

—*Thomas P. Ofcansky*
Washington, D.C. and London

Introduction

As the new century begins, it is evident that much of the world's wildlife could face extinction, largely because of an expanding human population and a high rate of industrial and agricultural development. Canada and the United States, for example, have lost many species of their native grazing animals to the forces of modernization. Even before 1900, European big game hunters, using primitive firearms, had changed the face of several African, Asian, and Latin American countries by exterminating millions of wild animals for food, profit, and sport; or, more importantly, to make way for farms, settlements, towns, and cities.

Although many individuals, organizations, and governments have tried to halt this destruction by supporting the enactment of game laws and the establishment of game reserves or national parks, the slaughter of wild animals continues. This crisis has been particularly acute throughout the savanna areas of eastern Africa where once thriving herds have been greatly reduced or have disappeared. Because the evolution of this region's ecological history during the past century has paralleled developments in other parts of the world, East Africa or more precisely Kenya, Uganda, and Tanganyika (now Tanzania)is a logical place to begin the study of man's impact on wildlife.

East Africa's geographic diversity offers the tourist a unique opportunity to participate in a wide variety of activities, including sport fishing in the Indian Ocean, climbing Mount Kenya or Kilimanjaro, or just enjoying the region's pleasant climate. The visitor also can see a fascinating array of African peoples, such as the Maasai warriors. Most tourists, however, travel to East Africa to look at one of the world's last great assemblages of wildlife. Indeed, more than 140 species of mammals may be found throughout East Africa, most of them small nocturnal creatures. Of the larger species the most familiar are the lion, elephant, buffalo, and rhinoceros.[1]

East Africa's human population has more than doubled in the past eighty years and threatens the future existence of these animals by placing ever increasing demands on the region's limited resources. Some of the factors involved in this dilemma include

---

[1]D.F. Horrobin, *A Guide to Kenya and Northern Tanzania* (New York: Charles Scribner's Sons, 1971), p. 183.

habitat destruction, poaching, and the unwillingness or inability of officials to enforce wildlife protection laws. Even when Kenya announced a total ban on hunting in 1977, many wildlife experts correctly predicted that the country's fauna would continue to decline.[2]

During the ensuing decades of British rule, several ecological issues confronted East Africa's colonial administrators. In Kenya, for example, an expanding European and African population battled wild animals for superiority over the land and its resources. A never-ending confrontation between elephant herds and African and European farmers was Uganda's main wildlife problem. The link between the tsetse fly and wild animals which caused an often fatal disease in man and his domestic stock persuaded many European settlers and officials in Tanganyika to demand the total destruction of all fauna. To make matters worse, as East Africa's indigenous population grew and firearms became more readily available, poaching took an increasing toll on the region's wildlife.[3]

On a broader level, the existence of large herds of wild animals throughout East Africa impeded the growth of a modern economy and advanced forms of production, health care, education, and transportation. Indeed, the commitment to game preservation, a concept with deep roots in the British experience, and the desire to develop East Africa along western lines, placed colonial administrators in the difficult position of trying to devise a land-use policy that would enable humans and animals to live side by side in relative peace and harmony without disturbing the region's economic growth. Appreciating this predicament is the key to understanding the disappearance of so much wildlife throughout East Africa and the world.

East Africa is a land of impressive proportions and variety. Its land mass covers approximately 683,000 square miles or about the combined area of the British Isles, France, Switzerland, Spain, and Italy. Of this, about 39,000 square miles are inland lakes, streams, and rivers. The region's geographical boundaries encompass some of the world's most beautiful territory. To the east is the Indian Ocean; to the south the 450-mile-long Ruvuma River; to the west a great crescent of lakes stretching from southwestern Tanzania to west-central Uganda; and to the north the Sudanese desert. Physiographical regions include coastal margins and the hinterland; alluvial basins; the plateaus of Maasailand, southeastern and central Tanzania, eastern and northern Kenya, and central Uganda; the Lake Victoria basin, the Rift Valley; and various mountains and mountain ranges.

---

2. J. Simpson, "The Great Kenya Wildlife Ripoff," *Field and Stream*, Vol. 82, No. 8 (December, 1977), p. 48.

3. The African poaching problem is discussed in N. Kelly, "In Wildest Africa: The Preservation of Game in Kenya, 1895 1933," (Ph.D. dissertation, Simon Fraser University, 1978).

No matter how impressive and awe inspiring these features may be, they cannot compare with East Africa's spectacular wildlife. In Kenya alone during the 1980s, the number of herbivores was approximately three million, mostly located in the country's many national parks and game reserves. Included in this group is the elephant which consumes up to a quarter of a ton of food per day; the rhinoceros, a beast whose foul nature reportedly stems from continual bouts of constipation; the giraffe, tallest of living quadrupeds; the hippopotamus, a strange-looking creature often weighing more than two tons; the zebra, a prodigious feeder which can eat an entire maize field in one night; the buffalo, an uncanny animal noted for its ability to kill unsuspecting hunters by doubling back on them; and the profusion of different antelope species.

Among the carnivora, the lion, symbol of British chivalry, courage, and power, is clearly one of the most dangerous predators in East Africa. Its mere presence has prevented mail deliveries, stopped railroad construction work, and terrorized isolated farms and settlements. Other carnivores include the cheetah, a beautifully spotted creature that can attain speeds of up to 75 miles-per-hour; the leopard, a nocturnal hunter rarely seen by humans; the hyena, a night stalker which will eat anything from carrion to leather shoes and chairs; the jackal, a small relatively harmless foxlike animal; and the serval, a wild cat which often mates with the common house cat.

East Africa also contains the more common primates, foremost of which is the baboon, a tough gregarious beast that travels in troops ranging from thirty to more than one hundred. Apart from the seldom seen gorilla and the various smaller monkeys, the only other primate of note is the blackfaced vervet monkey, a mischievous critter with an annoying habit of plaguing hotels and homes in search of a handout.

Additionally, there is an assortment of rarer animal species scattered throughout East Africa. The now extinct wild ass, for example, was indigenous to the desert region around Lake Turkana's northern shore. In Kenya, the bongo antelope is confined to Mount Kenya's bamboo forest, the Aberdare Mountains, the Cherengani Range, and the Mau Forest. The sitatunga, originally known as Speke's antelope or the marshbuck, frequents some of Lake Victoria's uninhabited Sese Islands, the shores of nearby Lake Nabugabo, and formerly European owned land in the Kitale area of western Kenya. The sable antelope is limited to the coastal area near the Kenya-Tanzania border. Thomas's kob, another antelope species, can be seen only on the shores of Lake Victoria and western Kenya's Nzoia River.

It is now difficult to determine the extent of East Africa's wildlife herds at the dawn of British rule. However, various colonial officials have tried. In 1902, Richard Meinertzhagen, an officer in the King's African Rifles, conducted a census between the Athi River train station and Nairobi, a distance of sixteen miles. He counted five rhinoceroses, eighteen giraffes, 760 wildebeests, 4,006 zebras, 845 Coke's hartebeests,

324 Grant's gazelles, 142 Thomson's gazelles, 46 impalas, 24 ostriches, 16 baboons, and 7 greater bustards.[4]

Sir Charles Eliot, Kenya's Commissioner from 1900 to 1904, spoke of having seen "miles of zebras" on favorable days. John A. Hunter, a Scottish immigrant who later worked for Kenya's Game Department, claimed he "went nearly mad with excitement watching the strange beasts" that dotted the open plains. On his first journey through East Africa, Alan Workman, later Uganda's Postmaster General, wrote that he "eagerly watched the well nigh constant procession of game." Even Theodore Roosevelt, who visited East Africa in 1909-10 after leaving the American presidency, was amazed to learn that there had been "quite a plague of wild beasts" in Nairobi shortly before his arrival[5].

Modern anthropological theory holds that man's first appearance on this planet was in East Africa. The research of archeologists L.S.B. Leakey and D.W. Phillipson, in particular, places man's entry into the area sometime during the Pliocene or Lower Pleistocene age. The absence of reliable records has made it nearly impossible to determine the size and scope of East Africa's early human population. Most experts agree, however, that prior to the colonial period the region contained fewer than ten million people.

With such a small population, it was highly unlikely that man could seriously disturb the balance of nature during the precolonial period. Africans who hunted normally used rudimentary weapons. The Ndorobo people, for example, killed elephants with an eight-foot-long poison-tipped spear made from the wood of the wild olive tree. The Turkana people caught the rhinoceros with a wheel trap, an apparatus three feet across with a rim of twisted rawhide. Spikes were attached to the circumference and the trap then was tied to a heavy log. When a rhinoceros stepped in the wheel, the spikes penetrated its leg and the hapless beast dragged the tree trunk until it died of exhaustion or was killed by bowmen. The coming of the Europeans to eastern Africa was the catalyst that changed this ecological balance.[6]

Modern Europe's contact with East Africa's fauna-rich interior began in the late 1840s with the explorations of two German missionaries, Ludwig Krapf and Johannes Rebmann. They were followed by individuals such as Richard Burton, John

---

4. R. Meinertzhagen, *Kenya Diary* 1902-1906 (Edinburgh: Oliver and Boyd, 1957), pp. 56. During a trip along the same route in 1979, the author only saw approximately 100 wild animals.

5. C. Eliot, *The East Africa Protectorate* (London: Frank Cass and Company, Ltd., 1966), pp. 264-5; J.A. Hunter, *Hunter* (New York: Harper and Brothers, 1952), pp. 189; A. Workman, *A Colonial Postmaster-General's Reminiscences* (London: Grayson and Grayson, 1937), p. 22; and T. Roosevelt, *African Game Trails* (New York: Scribners, 1910), p. 271.

6. Simon, *Sunlight and Thunder* p. 149.

Speke, and James Grant, and others, who generated popular interest with stories of plentiful wildlife, new discoveries, strange diseases, and human slavery. These factors, combined with Europe's growing nationalism, prompted several governments, the most successful of which was Great Britain, to engage in a scramble for East Africa territory.[7]

British colonialism in East Africa began in the second half of the nineteenth century when all the major European powers embraced imperialism as a matter of national pride and survival. This prompted an enormous public demand for information about the "Dark Continent." Explorers, such as twenty-four-year-old Joseph Thomson, the first European to travel from Zanzibar to Lake Victoria via Maasailand in 1884, brought back thrilling descriptions of East Africa's flora and fauna, and mysterious maps of its mountains, rivers, lakes, and jungles.[8]

The people of Great Britain also read about the region's grasslands and forests in such books as Captain James Grant's *A Walk Across Africa* (1864) or Charles New's *Life, Wanderings and Labours in Eastern Africa* (1873).[9] More importantly, these and scores of other books and articles contained tales of many different peoples—including the Chagga, Kamba, Kikuyu, and Baganda—who lived and worked in East Africa. Such stories attracted the attention and concern of missionaries eager to save millions of "heathen" souls; explorers hoping to gain immortality by discovering a previously unknown mountain or lake; big game hunters seeking an overnight fortune in ivory; politicians searching for overseas colonies; and, businessmen looking for new markets.

By the mid-1880s, the British and German governments had expressed an interest in East Africa's strategic and economic potential. As each government began to fear the ambitions of the other, the chances for conflict increased. To prevent open warfare, Great Britain and Germany signed an agreement in 1886 partitioning East Africa. The task of "opening up" the British territory fell to a small group of Manchester entrepreneurs who, under the leadership of Scottish shipping magnate Sir William Mackinnon, formed themselves into the British East Africa Association in 1885.[10]

Mackinnon's first accomplishment was to persuade the Sultan of Zanzibar to relinquish control of a ten-mile-wide coastal strip between the Umba River and Kipini,

---

7. For a classic examination of the British role in the scramble for eastern Africa, see R. Coupland, *The Exploitation of East Africa 1856-1890: The Slave Trade and the Scramble* (London: Faber and Faber, 1968).

8. J. Thomson, *Through Masai Land* (London: Samson Low, Marston and Company., 1887).

9. J.A. Grant, *A Walk Across Africa* (London: Blackwood, 1864); and C. New, *Life, Wanderings and Labours in Eastern Africa* (London: Hodder and Stoughton, 1873).

10. The best history of the Imperial British East Africa Company is J.S. Galbraith, *Mackinnon and East Africa 1878-1895* (Cambridge: Cambridge University Press, 1972).

a small harbor town south of Witu, to allow unrestricted access to the interior. In exchange for this concession, Mackinnon promised to administer the territory in the Sultan's name and provide him with 50 percent of any net revenues gained because of the agreement. Mackinnon and his associates quickly realized that it would be difficult to administer and develop East Africa's interior. To raise the capital necessary for such an undertaking, Mackinnon reorganized the Association into the Imperial British East Africa Company (IBEA) and secured a royal charter from the British government in 1888.[11] The charter empowered the IBEA to administer parts of the interior where it could acquire protection treaties approved by the Secretary of State for Foreign Affairs. The Company eventually established a string of fortified posts stretching from its Mombasa headquarters to Tsavo, Kibwezi, Machakos, Fort Smith, Njemps, Mumias, and onward to Uganda, a land supposedly "flowing with milk and honey."

Dr. Carl Peters, a German adventurer whose brutality among the African people had earned him the reputation of being Mkono wa Damu, "the man with blood on his hands," unwittingly aided the IBEA's territorial expansion.[12] In July 1889, he secretly landed in Witu and, with a small force, set out up the Tana River, ostensibly to relieve Emin Pasha, another German national who held the Egyptian governorship of Sudan's Equatorial Province and who had been cut off from the outside world by the 1883 Mahdist uprising. In fact, Peters intended to seize the hinterland behind Witu.

As part of his strategy he concluded a treaty with Kabaka Mwanga of Buganda in March 1890, which gave Germany equal trade rights with other European states. Peters hoped to use this agreement to extend German political control over the area of present-day Uganda and block British access to the country. Unfortunately for Peters, the East Africa question was ultimately settled in Europe without reference to the Buganda treaty or, for that matter, to the IBEA's activities.

On 1 July 1890, a second Anglo-German agreement ended the scramble for East Africa. It defined the boundary between the British and German protectorates, assigned Witu, Zanzibar, and Uganda to Great Britain, and awarded the North Sea island of Heligoland and a region west and south of Lake Victoria to Germany. Peters was so indignant that he criticized the German government for sacrificing two African kingdoms (Witu and Uganda) for a "bathtub in the North Sea."[13]

---

11. The text of the charter is contained in P.L. McDermott, *British East Africa or IBEA* (London: Chapman and Hall, 1895), pp. 476-85.

12. For a detailed biography of Peters, see H.M. Gair, "Carl Peters and German Colonialism," (Ph.D. dissertation, Stanford University, 1968).

13. Quoted in Z.A. Marsh and G.W. Kingsnorth, *An Introduction to the History of East Africa* (Cambridge: Cambridge University Press, 1965), p. 109.

Thus, by the end of the nineteenth century British rule in East Africa was beginning to take shape around IBEA activities. Following the Company's financial reversals in early 1893, the British government gradually assumed control of Uganda and Kenya. Tanganyika, now known as Tanzania, was acquired by the British after World War I. As the administering power, the IBEA and later the British government, were responsible for many activities, including game preservation—a most difficult task.

Throughout the colonial period, the British government and, to a lesser extent, the respective colonial administrations were committed to game preservation. That East Africa's fauna continued disappearing in ever-increasing numbers reflected not only man's hostility toward wildlife but also officialdom's inability to devise a policy that preserved wild animals without disturbing social and economic development. In Kenya, for example, colonial authorities attempted to formulate a scheme to protect wildlife and encourage widespread agricultural growth. Colonial policy-makers in Uganda attempted to design a plan to safeguard the country's elephants as well as the crops of African and European farmers. In Tanganyika, the government worked to eradicate the tsetse fly without destroying the wild animals that carried and transmitted the deadly trypanosomes from fly to man.

Although it is fashionable today to reject all forms of European imperialism, especially in Africa, a handful of colonial administrators fought valiantly against a staggering array of social, economic, political, and scientific problems to preserve East Africa's wildlife. That much of the region's fauna vanished during the colonial period while the remainder was confined in later years to artificially created game reserves or national parks is as much a condemnation of human nature as it is of a political system.

Man Versus Animal in the Garden of Eden: Kenya

Kenya was known as the East Africa Protectorate from 1895 to 1920. Throughout this period into 1945, the British colonial government sought to adopt a land-use policy that would preserve large numbers of wild animals without disturbing the country's economic development. However, this was to be an almost hopeless task, as Kenya's human population grew, and more territory came under cultivation by the British or was sacrificed for schools, hospitals, and towns. By 1945, it was evident to conservationists and politicians that all attempts to achieve these contradictory goals had failed and that a new approach was needed to assure the survival of Kenya's fauna. Even more disastrous, from an ecological point of view, were the far-reaching technological innovations that accompanied this population explosion.

The construction of the 584-mile long Uganda Railway from Mombasa to Port Florence (Kisumu) on the shores of Lake Victoria was the most significant event during the early years of colonial rule. By providing easy access to the interior, which contained some of Africa's richest game fields, the railroad enabled hunters and adventurers to upset the balance of nature that had existed for centuries. The establishment of a European farming community in Kenya's Highlands also altered the man-animal relationship.

Along with settlers anxious to start a new life, came all the accoutrements of western society, including farms, fences, towns, roads, schools, medicines, and hospitals. As Kenya became more modernized, many wildlife herds, which often traveled hundreds of miles to search for food and water, had to be reduced or eliminated. Thus, the problem confronting the colonial government was how to create a new ecological balance in a society committed to rapid economic development.

Kenya's colonial period can be divided into three phases. From 1888 to 1895, the Imperial British East Africa Company (IBEA) laid the foundation of British rule by securing control over an area of more than 300,000 square miles. During the Foreign Office's control of Kenya, 1895 until 1905,[a] the British government financed the Uganda Railway's construction and supported a scheme to transform Kenya into a "white man's country." Throughout the Colonial Office era, which began in 1905, Kenya's European population expanded and tried to transform the country into a modern nation state. During each stage, farmers and colonial administrators failed to resolve adequately the wildlife question.[1]

Game Policy Under the Imperial British East Africa Company, 1888-1895

The Imperial British East Africa Company (IBEA) based its game preservation policy on a combination of political, economic, and ecological considerations. Foremost was its desire to keep European sportsmen out of the interior for fear a clash with Africans might lead to a costly punitive expedition. Given that some of the Kamba and Kikuyu peoples had a reputation for attacking IBEA representatives and installations, this policy attracted little opposition.

Accordingly, on 19 June 1891, the IBEA requested the Foreign Office's approval to prohibit hunting and killing of game and to "interdict the passage of individuals or parties from the coast ports in search of sport." The hunting ban could be rescinded as soon as the Company had extended its authority over the interior, and shooting might be allowed in areas "infested to excess" with wildlife.[2]

Eight days later, the Foreign Office responded that Articles IX and X of the 1890 Brussels Act, which regulated the introduction of firearms into a large part of Africa, should

---

a. The British ruled their empire largely through the Colonial Office, which was established in 1854. However, the Foreign Office, which worked out of the same London office building as the Colonial Office, also administered several overseas colonies. On 1 April 1905, the Colonial Office, which had more resources than the Foreign Office, assumed responsibility for the East Africa Protectorate (now Kenya), Uganda, the British Central Africa Protectorate (now Malawi), and British Somaliland (now part of Somalia). Eventually, the Colonial Office established so-called unified branches of colonial government throughout the empire. These branches included the Administrative Service, Agricultural Service, Audit Service, Chemical Service, Civil Aviation Service, Customs Service, Education Service, Engineering Service, Forest Service, Geological Survey Service, Legal Service, Medical Service, Mines Service, Police Service, Postal Service, Prisons Service, Research Service, Veterinary Service, and Nursing Service. Conspicuous by its absence is a Wildlife Service.

1. The best account of the railway remains M.F. Hill, *Permanent Way*, Vol. I, 2nd Edition (Nairobi: East African Literature Bureau, 1976); the only scholarly history of the Imperial British East Africa Company is contained in J.S. Galbraith, *Mackinnon and East Africa 1878-1895* (Cambridge: Cambridge University Press, 1972); for an excellent study of early settler politics, see G.H. Mungeam, *British Rule in Kenya 1895-1912* (Oxford: Clarendon Press, 1966).

2. IBEA to FO, 19 June 1891, Foreign Office Confidential Print (hereafter FOCP) 6127/188. For an examination of Kamba and Kikuyu resistance, see R. Tignor, *The Colonial Transformation of Kenya: The Kamba, Kikuyu, and Maasai from 1900 to 1939* (Princeton: Princeton University Press, 1976), pp. 15-41.

form the basis of the IBEA's wildlife preservation policy. Under the terms of these clauses, the Company had the right to issue gun licenses. It also could ban big game hunting by publishing a notice that political problems in the interior prevented the issuance of licenses to European sportsmen.[3]

Although it adopted this strategy, the IBEA, with a European staff in Africa of only 117 men, was hardly in a position to prevent conflicts between Europeans and Africans or to enforce game regulations. In August 1892, for example, William Astor Chanler, a noted big game hunter, and Ludwig von Hohnel, a Hungarian adventurer, departed the coast to explore the upper Tana River. Upon reaching the river, Chanler realized that their supplies were dangerously low. When the Pokomo people, who resided in the area, refused to sell food, Chanler took some by force and then paid them. En route through the mountains northeast of Mount Kenya, Chanler and von Hohnel engaged in several battles with the Embu people. When they returned to Zanzibar, several porters accused Chanler of extreme cruelty and homicide.[4]

Other European sportsmen caused problems for the IBEA by their unwarranted excesses. In 1893, Garner Muir and his Scottish ghillie killed more than eighty rhinoceroses in the Machakos region in less than three months. The Company's directors reacted to this by implementing a £500 sporting tax on every European hunter. Unfortunately, this scheme failed to limit or control big game hunters, largely because the IBEA lacked the personnel to maintain an effective law enforcement system. On 10 February 1893, the directors, therefore, advised Ernest Berkeley, the Acting Administrator at Mombasa, to "do his best to collect the. . .fee."[5]

Sixteen months later, the IBEA issued more realistic sporting regulations based on those in force in the British Central Africa Protectorate. Under the new ordinance anyone entering the Company's territory to hunt elephant, rhinoceros, and the larger antelopes had to obtain a £25 license from the Administrator at Mombasa, or from the district superintendents at Wanga, Malindi, or Lamu. Moreover, the importation and use of firearms were subject to the terms of the General Act of the Brussels Conference. The IBEA also assessed a 15 percent duty on ivory and a 10 percent duty on rhinoceros horns and hippopotamus teeth. In addition, every sportsman had to deposit £100 as surety, which was returned when leaving the country, if the hunter had conformed to game regulations.

---

3. FO to IBEA, 27 June 1891, FOCP 6127/200; also, see Chanler to IBEA, 28 November 1892, enclosure in IBEA to FO, 7 February 1893, FO 2/97; and Chanler to IBEA, 28 November 1892, Mackinnon Papers, File 48.

4. Cracknall to FO, 13 April 1894, FOCP 6557/141.

5. Precis of Mails sent to Mombasa, 10 February 1893, Mackinnon Papers, File 53; also see, F.J. Jackson, *Early Days in East Africa* (London: Edward Arnold, 1930), pp. 288-9.

Finally, the Company reserved the right to fine any person a sum of not less than £50 for taking game without a license. The directors subsequently amended this ordinance to prohibit the killing of cow elephants, on penalty of a £10 fine and confiscation of all ivory.[6]

The Company also tried to improve its ailing financial condition by levying a 15 percent ivory export duty at Mombasa. Apart from forcing the IBEA into the position of advocating elephant conservation while at the same time encouraging ivory exports to increase revenue, this policy caused several arguments with coastal traders and the German East Africa colonial administration. Commercial firms such as Smith, Mackenzie and Company objected to paying an export duty in Uganda and another in Mombasa. The Germans complained that IBEA-sponsored ivory traders refused to pay duties at border check points, while private traders accused the Company of harassment and illegal ivory confiscations. Nevertheless, the following table shows that ivory export duties contributed substantially to the IBEA's treasury.[7]

TABLE I

IMPORTS OF IVORY TO ZANZIBAR

Year	Total Imports Value in £	Imports from Kenya in £	Percentage of Total	Imports from GEA in £
1892	148,495	23,153	15.5	116,169
1893	150,930	?	?	?
1894	142,181	20,975	13.75	121,567
1895	102,351	17,069	16.75	77,556

The IBEA period, therefore, was a time of confusion and uncertainty. Although the Company enacted the country's first sporting regulations, it lacked the means to administer them. Generally, the IBEA also supported elephant conservation but economic exigencies compelled its directors to act otherwise. Its performance could be seen as a policy of words without deeds. However, this criticism must be tempered by the realization that, for all its failings, the IBEA initiated the concept of modern game preservation in East Africa.

Game Policy Under the Foreign Office, 1895-1905

During the Foreign Office era of British rule, the wildlife question became a major political issue, largely because of England's commitment to game preservation which

6. IBEA to FO, 26 October 1894, FOCP 6661/82.

7. Examples of objections to the 15 percent export duty are contained in Evan Smith to FO, 28 January 1891, FOCP 6124/189; IBEA to FO, 7 August 1891, FOCP 6261/78; and Hardinge to FO, 13 November 1894, FOCP 6661/202. Also, see IBEA to FO, 19 June 1891, FOCP 6127/188; and Board of Trade to FO, 15 January 1900, FO 403/302.

stretched back to Norman times.[8] Given this legacy, it was inevitable that the future of Africa's fauna became a hotly debated issue in public and official circles long before the Foreign Office assumed administrative control of Kenya.

In 1857, for example, the noted explorer David Livingstone claimed that the continent's wildlife was melting away "like snow in the spring."[9] Fourteen years later, explorer Dr. Georg Schweinfurth warned of the elephant's imminent extermination in eastern Africa.[10] In 1890, Sir Charles Wentworth Dilke, former Under Secretary of State for Foreign Affairs, wrote that Kenya's ivory resources would disappear unless strict conservation measures were implemented.[11]

So, by the time the IBEA relinquished control of Kenya, British opinion already was partially mobilized in the cause of game preservation. As a reflection of this attitude, the semi-official *Gazette for Zanzibar and East Africa* criticized Kenya's newly-formed colonial administration for its lackadaisical attitude toward fauna:

> The devastation wrought by the rifle-bearing hunter, professional and amatuer. . .in the immense herds of big game which used to roam the Prairies and Forests of North America, is an object lesson which we in British East Africa should take to heart. There is ample evidence that the game of this country is going the way of that in America; and considering its commercial value. . .it would show lamentable lack of wisdom if measures were not shortly instituted with a view to game preservation.[12]

During this period, senior British government officials also were distressed about East Africa's fauna. On 27 May 1896, Prime Minister and Foreign Secretary Lord Salisbury, a wildlife enthusiast who thrilled to stories of man-eating lions along the Uganda Railway, communicated with Sir Arthur Hardinge, Kenya's Commissioner, about the "excessive destruction" of wild animals. Unless this slaughter was stopped, Salisbury believed, the country's fauna would disappear in a few years. He subsequently asked Hardinge about the extent to which old IBEA game regulations were being applied. Lastly, Salisbury wondered whether the wildlife problem could be resolved by enacting a close time (viz. periods

8. For an analysis of early British game preservation policies, see A.L. Poole, *From Domesday Book to Magna Carta 1087-1216* (Oxford: Clarendon Press, 1951); M. Powicke, *The Thirteenth Century 1216-1307* (Oxford: Clarendon Press, 1953); and C. Young, "Conservation Policies in the Royal Forests of Medieval England," *Albion* Vol. 10 No. 2 (1978), pp. 95-103.

9. David Livingstone, *Missionary Travels and Researches in South Africa* (London: John Murray, 1857), p. 152.

10. Georg Schweinfurth, *The Heart of Africa*, Vol II (London: Sampson Low, Marston, Low, and Searle, 1874), p. 24.

11. C.W. Dilke, *Problems of Great Britain*, Vol. II (London: Macmillan and Co., 1890), p. 170.

12. *The Gazette for Zanzibar and East Africa*, 25 September 1895, p. 3.

Like many colonial officials, Sir Hesketh Bell, governor of Uganda, 1907-1910, was an avid big-game hunter.

Courtesy of the Royal Commonwealth Society

during which all hunting was prohibited), creating game reserves, specifying bag limits, or levying a high license fee.[13]

Clifford Craufurd, Kenya's Acting Commissioner, responded to Lord Salisbury by submitting a series of draft game regulations. Craufurd pointed out that the colonial administration was conducting discussions with the Sub-Commissioners for Ukamba and Tanaland Provinces about the feasibility of declaring the entire Kenia District in the south-western portion of the country a game sanctuary. Furthermore, Craufurd maintained that local administrative officers could deal with the excesses of African hunters while "non-native" sportsmen would be subject to a £100 surety deposit and a £25 license fee. Animals that could be shot on this license included two each of the following: elephant, rhinoceros, hippopotamus, zebra, buffalo, warthog, giraffe, any antelope species, and an unlimited number of lion, leopard, hyena, and crocodile. This proposed ordinance also would have prohibited killing elephants with tusks under ten pounds each, and females and young of all species. Because of their status as vermin, female lions, leopards, hyenas, and crocodiles could be shot. Lastly, the regulations would have banned the use of game nets, fire, large-scale drives, and other "unsportsmanlike" hunting methods.[14]

---

13. Salisbury to Hardinge, 27 May 1896, FOCP 6849/175; copy in FO 403/302.

14. Craufurd to FO, 14 December 1896, FOCP 6951/36.

The lion is East Africa's most powerful flesh eater. With the exception of man, the lion has no natural enemy.

Courtesy of the author

Water Buffalo. When wounded, the Cape Buffalo, which lives throughout East Aftrica, has a reputation for savagery among big-game hunters all over the world.

Courtesy of the author

The heavily built wildebeest is preyed upon by lions, cheetahs, and wild dogs.

Courtesy of the author

The annual wildebeest migrtation in the Serengeti involves thousands of animals.

Courtesy of Gerald Rilling

The hippopotamus, which can weigh up to 5,800 pounds, inhabits streams, lakes, and ponds throughout East Africa.

Courtesy of Gerald Rilling

Francis Hall, a former IBEA official who had accepted employment with the colonial administration, complained that Craufurd's proposal to make the whole Kenia District a game sanctuary was "the most terrible news we have heard." It meant that government officials stationed in Kenia would be forced to apply for leave and travel outside the District to shoot.[15] Fortunately, these objections failed to stop the establishment of Kenya's first game reserve.

After a year's discussion between officials in London and Zanzibar, Hardinge persuaded the Foreign Office to accept a revised draft regulation "more favorable to wealthy sportsmen who bring money into the territory." The major change limited the numbers that could be killed on license only to elephant, rhinoceros, and giraffe. Hardinge believed this would make Kenya more desirable than German East Africa as a hunting ground.[16] The revenues gained from sale of additional hunting licenses would help to justify the preservation of Kenya's wildlife on economic grounds. Finally, the new ordinance, which the Foreign Office approved on 30 December 1897, created a game sanctuary, which included most of the Kenia District.[17]

---

15. Hall to Hall, 28 January 1897, Hall Papers, Rhodes House, Oxford.

16. Making Kenya a popular hunting ground concerned officials and citizens for years. For a later analysis of this issue, see *African Standard*, 23 May 1903, p. 2.

17. Salisbury to Hardinge, 23 February 1897, FOCP 6951/89; copy in FO 403/302; Hardinge to Salisbury, 26 April 1897, FOCP 6964/87; Hardinge to Salisbury, 27 April 1897, FOCP 7018/211; FO to Hardinge, 30 December 1897, FOCP 7032/181. A copy of the 1897 regulation is contained in FO 403/302; and E.N. Buxton, *Two African Trips* (London: Edward Stanford, 1902), pp. 141-52.

Africans with bush buck kill. Gerald Rilling, a big-game hunter, and his African guides pose over a bush buck.

Courtesy of Gerald Rilling

Within three months, these regulations had alienated large segments of Kenya's growing European community. On 2 February 1898, Hardinge bowed to popular pressure and requested that Uganda Railway employees be allowed to shoot without payment of the £25 license fee.[18] Next, he asked permission to authorize "settlers and missionaries" to kill a "limited" amount of game for food. Salisbury not only sanctioned both changes but also reduced the license fee for colonial officers to £3.[19]

To help offset administrative expenses, the colonial authorities enacted a new game ordinance in August 1899. It provided for a more complex licensing scheme. In place of the uniform £25 fee, the government issued separate licenses to sportsmen for 375 rupees and to government officials, settlers, and traders for 45 rupees (as of 1920, the rupee was worth 1s. 4d.). The regulations further stipulated that, unless sportsmen and colonial officials paid extra fees, they could kill only two each of the following: elephant, rhinoceros, hippopotamus, buffalo, and giraffe. Settlers, however, could shoot any game on their lands. Additionally, the statute increased the penalty for hunting in the Kenia reserve without a license from £5 to £50. The penalty for illegal shooting was fixed at a maximum of 500

---

18. Hardinge to Salisbury, 2 February 1898, FO 403/302.

19. Hardinge to Salisbury, 31 March 1898, FO 403/302; Salisbury to Hardinge, 18 March 1898, FO 403/302; Salisbury to Hardinge, 20 May 1898, FO 403/302.

rupees, or if more than two animals were involved, at a maximum of 200 rupees each. Violators could be imprisoned for up to two months. By October 1899, the Foreign Office had amended these regulations to contain further the activities of European hunters. Henceforth, each license holder had to submit game returns to the colonial authorities.[20]

This ordinance caused friction between the European settler community and the colonial administration. Under the terms of the 45-rupee non-native license, settlers were limited to hunting in their home district and were permitted to kill only four each of the more common antelopes. Traders, on the other hand, while restricted to the same bag limit, were allowed to shoot in any district. Moreover, the 45-rupee government official's license entitled the bearer to the same privileges granted under the 375-rupee sportsman's license.

The colonial authorities justified these differences by indicating that, because settlers usually killed "for the pot," there was no harm in setting a bag limit or confining their activities to one district.[21] Traders could hunt anywhere because they travelled through many districts in the course of a year. The concession granted to government officials was a perequisite to relieve the monotony and boredom of day-to-day life in lonely outposts.

Objections to these regulations arose partially because many settlers were keen on hunting while others killed wild animals—especially elephants—to supplement meager incomes.[22] More importantly, however, was the fact that scores of settlers refused to accept a law that protected highly destructive animals:

> The farmer whose fences were destroyed by elephant and buffalo, whose labour was menaced by rhino, whose livestock was eaten by lions and leopards, and whose crops were trampled and destroyed by herds of zebra, wildebeest and antelope of various kinds, could hardly be expected to limit his "take" to two or three individual animals.[23]

Sir Charles Eliot, Hardinge's successor who encouraged expansion of European settlement, tried to resolve this issue by asking the British government to liberalize the settlers' bag limit. The Foreign Office approved Eliot's scheme and introduced an amendment to the game ordinance whereby each colonist could shoot "not more than ten animals of any one species other than Grant's gazelle, Thomson's gazelle, Waterbuck, and Hartebeest."[24] Given the wildlife problems that confronted the European settlers, this amendment failed

---

20. FO to Craufurd, 11 August 1899, FO 403/302; FO to Craufurd, 6 October 1899, FO 403/302.

21. Lansdowne to Eliot, 11 June 1903, FO 403/355; Eliot to FO, 11 June 1903, FO 2/819.

22. H. Seaton, *Lion in the Morning* (London: John Murray, 1963), p. 24.

23. Elspeth Huxley to author, 11 September 1979, private correspondence in the author's possession.

24. Eliot to FO, 11 June 1903, FO 2/819; Eliot to Lansdowne, 4 September 1903, FO 2/819; FO to Eliot, 19 October 1903, FO 2/819.

Cheetah family feeding on Thoman's Gazelle.

to placate them. Indeed, it was only after the Colonial Office had assumed control of Kenya, in 1905, that the settlers succeeded in having the law changed to reflect what they felt were the realities of life in the East African bush.

Apart from playing a crucial role in the formulation and implementation of Kenya's early game ordinances, the Foreign Office attacked the problem of African wildlife preservation on the international level. On 8 September 1897, Lord Salisbury claimed the "assembling of a Conference" and the subsequent adoption of strict resolutions by the international community would be the only sure way of preserving Africa's wild animals.[25] He proposed such a conference be held in London in the spring of 1898. Because of the difficulties of arranging a meeting of this magnitude, it was not until April 1900 that representatives of Great Britain, France, Germany, Portugal, Italy, Spain, and the Congo Free State finally met for the first International Conference for the Preservation of the Wild Animals, Birds, and Fishes of the African Continent.

After two months of negotiations, the conference agreed to a convention that proposed to preserve Africa's fauna by implementing strict bag limits, establishing game sanctuaries, and authorizing closed seasons. Because Portugal and France refused to accept uniform export duties and export limitations on hides, skins, and horns, the convention never was ratified. Nevertheless, the British government incorporated the convention's principles into Kenya's game regulations.

---

25. FO to CO, 8 September 1897, FOCP 7018/123; also, see Salisbury to Lascelles, 3 March 1898, FOCP 7024/119.

A new ordinance, gazetted on 15 October 1900, increased all hunting fees. Henceforth, the colonial administration charged 750 rupees for a sportsman's license and 150 rupees for a settler's or a government official's license. The law permitted settlers to kill two hippopotamuses a year, several species of wild pig, and certain antelopes and gazelles up to a bag limit of five per month. The penalty for violations increased to 1,000 rupees and, in the case of multiple offenses, 500 rupees per animal.

The most important change, however, was the creation of two new game sanctuaries. The Northern Reserve stretched from the Uganda Protectorate's border to Marsabit, south to the Guaso Nyiro River, and then to the Lake Baringo area. The Southern Reserve adjoined the Uganda Railway in the north, the German East Africa border in the south, the Uganda Protectorate in the west, and the upper Tsavo River in the East. The ordinance abolished the old Kenia District Reserve.[26]

In addition to the Foreign Office's international activities, a group of private English citizens, headed by Edward Buxton, a former big game hunter, championed the cause of transnational wildlife preservation. On 11 December 1903, Buxton launched the Society for the Preservation of the Wild Fauna of the Empire (hereafter referred to as the Fauna

Until recently, scientists believed the hyena was a scavenger. In fact it is one of East Africa's most fearsome hunters.

Courtesy of the author

---

26. A copy of the 1900 Game Ordinance is contained in CO 457/1. For a discussion of the enforcement of these regulations in the African communities, see Jackson to Sub-Commissioner, Fort Hall, 7 February 1907, Kenya National Archives (hereafter KNA): unnumbered circular.

Preservation Society). Its purpose was to collect information on the number of wild animals killed each year throughout the British Empire and to take all necessary steps to check this destruction.[27]

It also sought "...to create a sound public opinion on the subject at home and in our Dependencies, further the formation of game reserves and sanctuaries, the selection of the most suitable places for these sanctuaries, and the enforcing of suitable game laws and regulations."[28] By the end of its first year, the Fauna Preservation Society had seventy ordinary and thirty honorary members, and by 1904, it had begun publication of an annual journal. These accomplishments formed the nucleus of a highly influential political pressure group which, by the time of the Colonial Office's takeover of Kenya, exerted considerable influence over the country's wildlife preservation policy.

In the final analysis, the effectiveness of wildlife policies enacted from 1895-1905 depended upon the colonial administration's willingness and ability to enforce them. Unfortunately, the British government was in no mood to increase imperial expenditures, especially for something it viewed as eccentric as preserving wild animals in Kenya. Consequently, the official policy, as enunciated by Sir John Kirk, the retired Consul General of Zanzibar, was to establish vast game reserves and leave them unpoliced.[29]

Even the Foreign Office realized that a credible enforcement system was needed if the principles set forth in the 1900 international conference were to be carried out successfully. It therefore suggested to Hardinge that some experienced officer might "devote attention" to the matter. Subsequently, the colonial administration assigned Richard Crawshay the task of policing Kenya's two game reserves, which totaled more than 48,000 square miles, a region approximately the size of England.

There was very little one individual could hope to accomplish in such a vast area. Following the Foreign Office appointment of A. Blayney Percival as Game Ranger in 1901, the situation remained unsettled. Indeed, in his first report, Percival complained that only "a considerable force of police or scouts" could prevent breaches of the game ordinance.[30] Eliot, who resigned in 1904 because of a dispute with the British government over his pro-settler policies, sympathized with Percival's plight:

---

27. R. Fitter and P. Scott, *The Penitent Butchers* (London: Fauna Preservation Society, 1978), p. 8. After World War I, the society changed its name to the Society for the Preservation of the Fauna of the Empire. In 1950, it became the Fauna Preservation Society. For sake of clarity and consistency, Fauna Preservation Society will be used throughout the text.

28. *Journal of the Society for the Preservation of the Wild Fauna of the Empire*, Vol II (1905), p. 1.

29. Sir John Kirk's memorandum, dated 31 July 1897, is contained in FO 403/302.

30. A.B. Percival, Report on East Africa Game Reserve, enclosure #1 in Eliot to Lansdowne, 10 December 1901, FO 2/818.

> Even among average law-abiding citizens there is a feeling that game regulations, like customs regulations, belong to that class of enactments which have no moral force, and may be violated without loss of moral character when they can be violated with impunity.[31]

Ensuring African compliance with game regulations was even more difficult. According to Hardinge:

> Most of these tribes are. . .too primitive to be made to comprehende [sic] or apply a system of game licenses, and too nomadic for it to be possible without a force of police throughout their countries, the size and cost of which would be out of proportion to the end in view.[32]

Frederick C. Selous, a noted big game hunter, supported Hardinge's assessment and advised Lord Salisbury that controlling African hunters would be a "difficult matter."[33]

The Foreign Office era, therefore, witnessed the many wildlife preservation advances, including the 1900 international conference, the creation of two game reserves, and the appointment of a full-time Game Ranger. On the negative side, little was done to establish an effective policing system. This is not to suggest that the colonial administration neglected the country's ecological well-being. On the contrary, the Foreign Office's achievements can be appreciated only when examined against the backdrop of the political and economic problems plaguing the British in East Africa during those years. Many areas of Kenya were still being brought under British administration. In Jubaland, the Northern Frontier District, and portions of western Kenya, for example, the British presence amounted to little more than a few fortified stations or trading posts. Until the British pacified these areas, the danger of violence or open revolt was a constant threat. Moreover, the cost of administering territories already controlled by the government increased so rapidly that, from 1895 to 1905, the British Treasury gave grants-in-aid totalling no less than £1,656,408 to the fledgling governments.[34] In such an atmosphere it was hardly reasonable to expect that vast sums of money would or could be spent on preserving wild animals and their habitats.

---

31. Charles Eliot, *The East Africa Protectorate* (London: Frank Cass and Co. Ltd., 1966), p. 276.

32. Hardinge to FO, 21 March 1900, FOCP 7405/30.

33. F.C. Selous, undated memorandum contained in British Plenipotentiaries to the Game Conference to Salisbury, 21 May 1900, FO 403/303; also, see Sclater to Hill, 27 December 1899, FO 403/302.

34. Great Britain, *Reports Relating to the Administration of the East Africa Protectorate*, Cd. 2740 (1905), p. 44.

Game Policy Under the Colonial Office, 1905-1963

On 1 April 1905, the Colonial Office assumed control of Kenya and the Protectorates of Uganda, Central Africa, and British Somaliland.[35] Even before this takeover, the land-use conflict between European settlers and proponents of the country's wildlife had reached the critical stage. As indicated by the following poem, which appeared in the *African Standard* in 1903, many settlers were bitterly opposed to game regulations and wildlife preservation:

THE EAST AFRIACAN MENAGERIE
(Inspired on Reading the East Africa Game Regulations)

You pay your money, in you come,
And walk around the show
You pitch your tent and take your pick
And aprospecting go.

While you're away a hippo comes,
A smelling round for roots,
He sees your tent and eats in up,
But woe to him who shoots.

You place your billie on the ground
And leave it in your rear
An ape he comes and rips it off,
But you mustn't shoot the dear.

A Mighty Tusker strolls along,
And thinks he'd like some fun,
You drop your pick and run like mad,
But you mustn't use your gun.

You turn to camp in dead disgust
And what do you see en route;
But a rhino goring your boy
But my, you daren't shoot.

---

35. For Original Correspondence on the Handover of the Protectorate 1904-1905, see CO 519/1.

And when your near starvation point
With rations down to half
You daren't shoot an antelope,
Much less a young giraffe.

A rich man's park's no place for me
So I give myself a boot
Back to the White man's land in the South,
Where it isn't a crime to shoot.[36]

After 1905, settler complaints about wild animals continued unabated. To protect crops and valuable water supplies from the ravages of zebras, wildebeests, hartebeests, elands, and gazelles, many farmers erected barbed wire fences at a cost of approximately £40 per mile. These failed to deter a thirsty rhinoceros, or a hungry gazelle that jumped four-or five-foot fences with ease, or a frightened zebra herd stampeded by lions.[37]

For those who failed to build fences for economic reasons, matters were even worse. A single wildebeest herd could eat fifty acres of wheat in a night. One planter reported that Thomson's gazelles and hartebeests consumed ten acres of beans while another complained that zebras and hartebeests destroyed fifty acres of young sisal plants. On one plantation, baboons cleared an entire maize field within a few days.[38]

Despite this destruction, the Fauna Preservation Society and, to a lesser extent, the British government remained committed to game preservation. The colonial administration—responsible for economic development as well as the safety of the country's fauna—usually vacillated between these two extremes. Indeed, throughout the 1905-1939 period, colonial authorities were in the untenable position of trying to pacify settlers by encouraging modernization and appeasing the Fauna Preservation Society and British government by preserving wildlife, a difficult undertaking.

To resolve this dilemma, Edward Buxton launched a campaign to pressure the British government into adopting a stronger fauna preservation policy. In the 1905 issue of the *Journal of the Society for the Preservation of the Fauna of the Empire*, he included an article

---

36. *African Standard*, 13 June 1903, p. 2.

37. J. Bland-Sutton, *Man and Creatures in Uganda* (London: Hutchinson and Company, 1933), pp. 161-2; L. Cone and J. Lipscomb, *A History of Kenya Agriculture* (Nairobi: University Press of Africa, 1972), p. 38; and Elspeth Huxley, *White Man's Country*, Vol. I (London: Chatto and Windus, 1974), pp. 161-2.

38. Detailed Account of the Damage Done by Game to Farmers in the Machakos and Part of Nairobi District, undated memorandum, enclosure #3 in Girouard to Harcourt, 6 June 1911, CO 885/20; C. Scott, "Game and Settlement in Kenya," *United Empire*, Vol. XXVIII No. 2 (February, 1937), pp. 72-3; and V.M. Carnegie, *A Kenya Farm Diary* (London: Blackwood, 1930), p. 58.

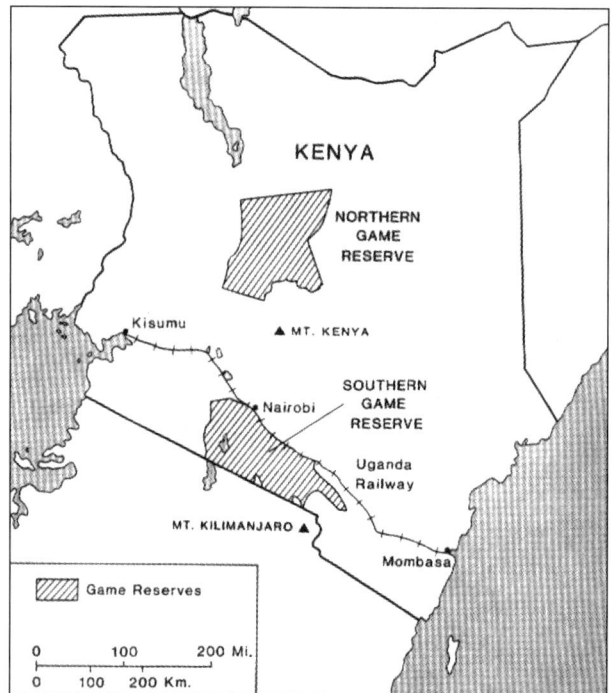

by Lord Hindlip, an influential Kenya settler, who argued for increased government expenditure for wildlife conservation.[39]

Then, on 2 February 1905, a Fauna Preservation Society deputation visited the Secretary of State for the Colonies, Alfred Lyttelton. Buxton, echoing Hindlip's sentiments, told Lyttelton that in Kenya "a very considerable revenue is derived from the game, to put it on the lowest ground—from the licence—and nothing like that sum is spent on preserving it." Additionally, Buxton maintained that game reserves should be established in areas where it was possible to enforce game regulations.[40]

Lyttelton responded by advising East Africa's Commissioners that:

> I stated that I did not think that there was any chance at the present moment of obtaining any contribution from the Imperial Exchequer in aid of the establishment of game reserves. I agreed that the reserves should be brought, where feasible, along the navigable rivers or railways. . . and that their size should be so restricted as to give them a fair chance of being effective.[41]

39. Lord Hindlip, "Preservation of the Fauna of British East Africa From the Point of View of a Settler," *Journal of the Society for the Preservation of the Wild Fauna of the Empire*, Vol. II (1905), pp. 51-7.

40. Great Britain, *Correspondence Relating to the Preservation of Wild Animal in Africa*, Cd. 3189 (1906), pp. 250-1.

41. Lyttelton to the Commissioners of the East Africa, Uganda, and Somaliland Protectorates, 1 June 1905, CO 879/87.

Thus, although Buxton failed to persuade the British government to allocate funds for additional reserves, he succeeded in initiating action whereby existing sanctuaries were reduced to more manageable proportions. The Northern Reserve's case was typical of the difficulties encountered during this process.

When the colonial administration established the Northern Reserve, it hoped to prevent European sportsmen from ravaging wildlife and to eliminate political problems with the local inhabitants.[42] The sanctuary was located in what would become the Northern Frontier Province, a sparsely populated semi-desert area of more than 125,000 square miles bordering Ethiopia and Sudan. Due to the lack of adequate grazing grounds, the reserve contained a small fauna population, which included elephant, rhinoceros, buffalo, giraffe, eland, greater and lesser kudu, impala, Waller's gazelle, and several lesser antelope.

After establishing control over this desolate region, the colonial administration took steps in 1908 to reduce the Northern Reserve "from its present unwieldly size."[43] As practically nothing was known about the variety and quantity of game in the sanctuary, Kenya's Lieutenant Governor, Frederick Jackson, dispatched John H. Patterson—who had helped build the Uganda Railway and had been appointed Principal Game Ranger in 1907—to the area to mark out new boundaries and conduct a game census.

Illness forced Patterson back to Nairobi just after he had demarcated the Urray Mountains, north of Marsabit, as the reserve's eastern border. Jackson, incensed by Patterson's failure to complete the mission, filed an unflattering minute on 1 July 1908:

> His report gives little or no information about the game that we did not know before, and we are still in ignorance regarding the variety and approximate quantity of game between Patterson's suggested boundary and the Laikipia escarpment.[44]

By August 1908, however, Jackson, a naturalist in his own right, had decided that "though our information is scanty, we know enough about the game to warrant our dealing with this reserve." He proposed "to cut the Rift Valley portion north of Lake Baringo, and make the Laikipia Escarpment and Mount Nyiro the western boundary; and reduce the eastern portion by one degree of longitude." Kenya's 1909 Game Ordinance redefined the reserve's boundaries according to Jackson's suggestions, thereby leaving a region of about 13,000 square miles.[45]

---

42. J.H. Patterson, *In the Grip of the Nyika* (London: Macmillan and Co. Ltd., 1910), p. 123.

43. Sadler to Crewe, 29 August 1908, in Great Britain, *Further Correspondence Relating to the Preservation of Wild Animals in Africa*, Cd. 4472 (1909), p. 95; also, see F.J. Jackson, Memorandum on the Game Ranger Report Ending 31 March 1906, enclosure #2 in CO 533/17.

44. Minute by F.J. Jackson, 6 June 1908, enclosure in Sadler to Crewe, 1 July 1908, CO 533/45.

45. A copy of the 1909 Game Ordinance is contained in CO 533/64.

John Boyes (left) and A.B. Percival. Boyes, the self-acclaimed "King of the Wakikuyu" and Percival pose for a rare photograph.

Courtesy of M.D. Kummerfeldt

A.B. Percival. In 1941, Percival became Ranger of Preserves in the East African Protectorate (now Kenya). Over the next several years, he worked in a variety of positions. In 1915, he became Kenya's Game Warden.

Courtesy of M.D. Kummerfeldt

J.H. Patterson became one of East Africa's most celebrated personalities after he shot two man-eating lions which had halted construction work on the Uganda Railway. In 1907 he became Kenya's Principal Game Ranger.

Courtesy of the Royal Commonwealth Society

In addition, this ordinance consolidated the Southern Reserve. According to recommendations made by Jackson and Sir James Hayes-Sadler, Kenya's governor, the sanctuary was reduced "by the area between the [Uganda] Railway and the Kyulu Hills from the Kiboko or Makindu to the Tsavo." Colonial authorities also said that the reserve's eastern boundary might be moved if game preservation interfered with the operations of a proposed sanseviera fibre industry.[46]

Apart from making the reserves more manageable, the 1909 regulations formalized the principle whereby game sanctuaries could be created, decreased or increased in size, or abolished altogether:

> The governor, with approval of the Secretary of State may by Proclamation declare any other portion of the Protectorate to be a game reserve, and may define or alter the limits of any game reserve, and this ordinance shall apply to every such game reserve.[47]

Buxton, who watched events in East Africa with great interest, used his organization to pressure the British government into expanding Kenya's Game Department. In 1906,

---

46. Sadler to Crewe, 29 August 1908, and enclosure #1 in Cd. 4472, pp. 95, 97.

47. 1909 Game Ordinance, CO 533/64.

two colonial government officers joined Buxton's campaign in an unofficial capacity. On 16 February, Jackson claimed that:

> The [Game] Department consisting as it does at present, of Mr. Percival, the Ranger, and four or six native scouts is considered. . .to be little more than a farce. This I submit, is no fault of Mr. Percival. . .Even if Mr. Percival had more funds at his disposal for an increased staff of native scouts, they would be of little use without European supervision. If the question is to be taken up seriously with a view to preserving the game from extinction within the decade or two. . .an adequate and properly organized game ranger's Department should be established without further delay.[48]

Seven months later, Sadler submitted a detailed report to the British government in which he outlined the probable cost of a Game Department.

1 Ranger	£600
1 Senior Assistant	£300
2 Assistants.....£250 each	£500
Horse and Travelling Allowance	£325
Native Scouts	£200
Rewards and Incidental Expenses	£500
Total	£2,425[49]

In view of Sadler's support and the fact that, since 1904, revenue derived from game licenses and fines amounted to £13,236 while expenditures were only £242, the British government allocated £2,300 in late 1906 for the creation of a Game Department. Early in the following year, the colonial administration established a four-man Game Department with Lieutenant Colonel John H. Patterson as Principal Game Ranger, A. Blayney Percival as Senior Assistant Game Ranger, and Charles J. Ross and G.H. Goldfinch as Assistant Game Rangers.

Until 1923, a variety of personnel, financial, and political problems limited the Department's effectiveness. Within seven months of his appointment, for example, Patterson was invalided to England, thereby reducing the Department to three men. In 1909, the colonial administration appointed a temporary assistant and assigned Percival to the post of Acting Game Ranger. Finally, in October 1910, the Department acquired a permanent Game Ranger, R.B. Woosnam, and a fifth European officer, C.W. Woodhouse. Unfortunately,

---

48. F.J. Jackson, untitled memorandum, 16 February 1906, enclosure #1 in Sadler to Elgin, 12 March 1906, Cd. 3189, pp. 340-1.

49. Sadler to Elgin, 24 September 1906, CO 533/17; copy in Cd. 4472, p. 7.

with the outbreak of the First World War, the Department virtually ceased to exist after the local authorities had drafted all five officers into the intelligence service. In 1915, the Department resumed operations on a limited basis with Goldfinch and a reduced staff of African scouts. On 4 June 1915, Woosnam was killed in action at the Dardanelles, and his post remained vacant until Percival became Game Warden in 1919.[50]

For several years, Percival struggled unsuccessfully to regain a full complement of European officers, and in his last report, written in 1922, he accused the colonial administration of playing politics with the Game Department:

> The remnant of the Game Department, despoiled of the hardly collected [sic] transport mules etc. by military necessity during the war and later when permission to expend the money received for mules etc. from the military on a Motor Car [sic], the car commandered [sic] and sold; personnel cut down til during 1923 the Department will probably consist of one man sitting in an office. I am of the opinion that it was false economy to cut down the Game Department expenditure to the extent it has been.[51]

Despite this pessimistic assessment, the appointment of Archie Ritchie—the acknowledged "grand old man" of game preservation—as Game Warden, in late 1923, gave the Game Department a new lease on life. Unlike his two predecessors, Ritchie had a scientific background, having earned an honors degree in zoology from Magdalen College, Oxford. According to Charles Pitman, Uganda's chief Game Warden from 1925 to 1950, Ritchie used this influence to wage a one man "diplomatic guerrilla action against small-minded officials who tried, time and again, to clip the wings of the Kenya Game Department."[52]

By 1925, Ritchie had succeeded in restoring the Game Department to its pre-war strength. Four years later, he acquired two European game control officers. Throughout the 1930s, Ritchie usually had at his disposal four European officers and one full-time game control officer. He also persuaded the colonial administration to increase the Game Department's budget from £7,237 in 1925 to £12,557 in 1929.[53] Unfortunately, these advances failed to improve the Department's overall operating capabilities.

As late as 1936, the Department discharged its duties with the same number of

---

50. Woosnam's obituary is contained in *Journal of the East Africa and Uganda Natural History Society*, Vol. V No. 10 (June, 1916), pp. 129-30. Percival's appointment was retroactive to 1915.

51. Colony and Protectorate of Kenya, *Game Department Annual Report 1922* (Nairobi: The Government Printer, 1923).

52. Bruce Kinloch, *The Shambaa Raiders* (London: Collins, 1972), pp. 95, 103.

53. Colony and Protectorate of Kenya, *Game Department Annual Report 1925* (Nairobi: The Government Printer, 1926), p. 6; and Colony and Protectorate of Kenya, *Game Department Annual Report 1936* (Nairobi: The Government Printer, 1937), p. 8.

European officers as it had done during the pre-World War I period, despite the fact that its mission had grown to include game control and the scientific study of wild animals. Moreover, the Department's budget remained constant even though its revenue increased from an average of £4,934 annually during the years from 1904 to 1914 to an annual average of £11,510 during the 1926-1936 decade. The colonial administration's penury caused Ritchie to say his main problem was "how to show champagne results on a beer budget."[54]

Nevertheless, he worked tirelessly to create a more stable man-animal balance, although the country's growing European and African population made it difficult. As wildlife related problems intensified, the Department's reputation deteriorated, causing Ritchie to observe:

> It is with the greatest reluctance that a body of the community will cease to look upon the Game Department as other than a source of arbitrary interference with the just rights and liberties of the individual, appearing to consider that game is preserved for the benefit of the Department. It must be the constant endeavour of this Department. . .to impress upon every person that the game belongs to them primarily, to the world more generally, and by reversion, to posterity.[55]

The Department's inability to resolve this conflict threatened Kenya's wildlife with extinction.

Predators presented one of the greatest obstacles to profitable farming and ranching. Leopards usually snapped up guard dogs and sheep that were left out at night. Hyenas, East Africa's greatest scavengers, ate thousands of head of stock annually, especially sheep. Lions were a special scourge; one report indicated that a settler could expect to lose at least 5 percent of his stock annually to these beasts. Understandably, many farmers had a harsh attitude toward wildlife. Some even advocated the extermination of the country's fauna for the sake of economic development.[56]

Ritchie believed there were three ways to prevent man-animal clashes—drive fauna out of agricultural areas, instill within each animal or herd respect for man and his property, or exterminate wildlife on a local basis. On the basis of these points, Ritchie formulated a "game control" policy:

---

54. East Africa Protectorate, *Annual Report of Game Warden 1913-14* (Nairobi: The Government Printer, 1915), p. 2; Colony and Protectorate of Kenya, *Game Department Annual Report 1931* (Nairobi: The Government Printer, 1932); and *Game Department Annual Report 1936*, p. 8.

55. A.T.A. Ritchie, Introductory Note, Hunter by J.A. *Hunter* (New York: Harper and Brothers, 1952), p. xi.

56. E. Brodhurst-Hill, *The Youngest Lion* (London: Hutchinson and Co., 1934), p. 42; T.C. Bridges, *Wardens of the Wild* (London: G.G. Harrap and Co., 1937), pp. 84-5; W.S. Bromhead, *What's What in Kenya Highlands* (Nairobi: The East African Standard Ltd., 1923), p. 12; *The Leader of British East Africa*, 7 December 1918, p. 1; and J.T. McCutcheon, *In Africa* (Indianapolis: Bobbs-Merrill, 1910), p. 245.

. . .an essential corollary of Game Preservation; for no human community will tolerate in its vicinity the existence of—much less subscribe to the protection of—species that are a perpetual source of danger or depredation; and if any general system of preservation is to persist, active intervention must always be ready at hand.[57]

The first two alternatives were little more than stop-gap measures. Animals driven out of a particular region usually returned, especially if food and water were available; and most species were incapable of learning "discipline and respect," no matter what the inducement or penalty.[58] Game control, therefore, was the only realistic course of action, and, from the mid-1920s onward, officials used it with increasing regularity. In 1924, for example, the Game Department furnished 20,000 rounds of ammunition to five African game scouts and dispatched them to the Uasin Gishu Plateau in northwestern Kenya. Since the early 1900s, Afrikaner settlers from South Africa had battled the plateau's wildlife for control of its limited resources. Ritchie hoped the African scout expedition would resolve the problem permanently. By the end of 1924, the scouts had killed approximately 4,000 zebra, one of Africa's greatest crop destroyers. Although this was only a tiny fraction of the zebra population, such constant harassment kept most of them away from farms.

The voracious zebra always has posed a threat to farmers' crops.

Courtesy of the author

---

57. Ritchie, Introductory Note, *Hunter*, pp. xi-xii.

58. Interview with R.M. Bere, 28-9 July 1979 (Bude, United Kingdom).

The Game Department recouped some of the operation's cost by selling each hide for three shillings. This trade became so profitable that, by 1925, the price had risen to ten shillings per hide. When the authorities permitted private citizens to sell hides at this price, scores of settlers joined in the slaughter. Consequently, by the end of 1926, the zebra had almost vanished from the plateau.[59]

In 1933, however, H.G. Evans, District Commissioner from Uasin Gishu, reported that game once again was causing "a lot of damage to young wheat." The District Council, the settlers' local government body, appealed to the Game Department for assistance. When the Department failed to take action, the District Council decided to shoulder "the responsibility of evolving suitable measures to combat incursion by game," adopting a "controlled shooting" policy which improved the situation considerably.[60]

In all fairness to the European settler, it should be pointed out that many large landowners maintained wildlife sanctuaries on their own land. Some of Kenya's most inviolable game reserves were on private property.[61] Even during the height of Uasin Gishu's wild animal difficulties, E.L.B. Anderson, the District Commissioner, reported that wealthy farmers regarded game as a natural asset to the plateau.[62]

Apart from carrying out "game control" schemes throughout Kenya, the Game Department acted as the government's land clearing agent in the late 1920s and early 1930s. John A. Hunter, first employed by the Department as an Elephant Control Officer in June 1927, participated in a clearing project in Machakos District east of Nairobi. According to Hunter, the Kamba community had increased at least sixfold since the advent of colonial rule while the rhinoceros population had grown to such an extent that they "disputed the natives' existing huts and crops." Ritchie dispatched Hunter to the area to eliminate this threat, and in three months he killed 163 of the beasts. After his return to Machakos, Hunter reflected on man's destructiveness:

> We could walk freely through the bush now for there was little chance of meeting a rhino. Walking in single file, we topped a little rise. I stopped in astonishment. Three months before we had crossed the same country that lay before us. Then it had been a maze of thorn bush and acacia, cut

---

59. This section is based on information contained in Colony and Protectorate of Kenya, *Game Department Annual Report 1924* (Nairobi: The Government Printer, 1925); *Game Department Annual Report 1925*; Colony and Protectorate of Kenya, *Game Department Annual Report 1926* (Nairobi: The Government Printer, 1927); Uasin Gishu District Annual Reports 1924, 1925, 1926; and the Usain Gishu District Political Record File—Game, KNA: PC/RVP 2/8/7, 9-19; and DC/UG/2/1.

60. Uasin Gishu District Annual Reports 1933, 1935, 1936, 1937, and 1938, KNA: PC/RVP 2/8/7, 9-19.

61. Interview with Hugh Lamprey, 14 June 1979 (Nairobi, Kenya); Uasin Gishu District Annual Report, 1936.

62. Hunter, *Hunter*, pp. 166-7, 189-90.

by a tangle of narrow rhino trails. Now it lay bare as a polished table. . . labor gangs had been moving steadily behind us, cutting down the bush and clearing the land. What a short time before had been as wild a bit of Africa as God ever made was now farming country. Not a tree or bush remained. Now that the scrub was gone, I could see the white network of rhino trails criss-crossing over the whole land. Already the grass was beginning to obliterate them. The freakish beasts that had traveled those trails for centuries were now dead and gone.[63]

Rhinoceros. The demand for its horn, which is used in the Orient for medical purposes and in Yemen for dagger handles, has brought the once prolific rhinoceros to the verge of extinction throughout East Africa.

Courtesy of the author

The 1929-1939 decade was a time of ambiguous successes for the Game Department. Ritchie ensured that the Department usually operated with a full complement of European officers. However, he failed to command a greater share of the colonial administration's financial resources, partially because of public hostility toward wild animals. He achieved a *modus vivendi* of sorts with the European settlers and the African community by implementing a "control" program, which only further reduced Kenya's rapidly diminishing wildlife. Lastly, Ritchie was unable to resolve the problem of preserving fauna in a society committed to rapid economic development. On a broader level, Ritchie was a farsighted official who repeatedly argued for the establishment of a national park system to preserve Kenya's wild animals.[64]

---

63. Kinloch, *Shambaa Raiders*, p. 101; Noel Simon, *Between the Sunlight and the Thunder* (Boston: Houghton Mifflin Company, 1963), p. 15.

64. Interview with Noel Simon, 14 May 1979 (London, United Kingdom).

CHAPTER II

The Elephant is
Lord of the Jungle: Uganda

In contrast to Kenya, the ecological situation in Uganda revolved around a single issue. The introduction of game preservation laws in the last years of the nineteenth century led to an elephant population explosion. The beasts raided and damaged an ever-increasing number of European plantations as well as the far more numerous African shambas (cultivated areas) looking for food and water. Particularly vulnerable were plantations and shambas on the edge of inhabited areas, or in isolated locations. "Dirty, unweeded, over-grown plantations and banana patches" also attracted hungry elephants each normally consuming five to six hundred pounds of food per day.[1]

As in Kenya, the British government evinced an early interest in preserving Uganda's wild animals, including the elephant. In 1896, Lord Salisbury dispatched the following communication to Sir Ernest Berkeley, the country's Commissioner and Consul-General:

> My attention has recently been called to the excessive destruction, by travellers and others in East Africa, of the larger wild animals generally known as "big game." There is reason to fear that unless some check is imposed upon the indiscriminate slaughter of these animals, they will, in the course of a few years, disappear from the British Protectorate.
>
> I am not aware how far the enclosed Regulations for sporting licences, issued by the Imperial British East Africa Company have even been applied, and it is obviously difficult to ensure the observance by parties inland of regulations affecting the killing of game. It is eminently desirable, however, that some steps should be taken, and I have, therefore, to request that you will furnish me with a report on the subject. It will be for your

---

1. R.M. Laws, I.S.C. Parker, R.C.B. Johnstone, *Elephants and Their Habitats: The Ecology of Elephants in North Bunyoro, Uganda* (Oxford: The Clarendon Press, 1975), p. 173; C.W. Hobley, "The London Convention of 1900," *Journal of the Society for the Preservation of the Fauna of the Empire*, New Series Part XX (August, 1933), p. 35; Uganda Protectorate, *Annual Report Game Department 1925* (Entebbe: The Government Printer, 1926), p. 15; C.R.S. Pitman, Elephant Control: In Operation, Pitman Papers, Museum of Natural History Library, Z 89 FP #3, pp. 2-3.

consideration whether it would be advisable to deal with the question to some extent by establishing a close time, by specifying reserved districts, and by limiting the number of any particular class of game to be shot by an individual sportsman.

In any case a regulation should be issued, if not already in force, requiring persons, intending to shoot big game for sporting purposes, to take out a licence, the fee for which should be sufficiently high to serve as a check. In British Central Africa the cost of a licence is £25.[2]

Approximately six months later, Berkeley responded to Salisbury by submitting a series of draft game regulations based upon what seemed to be the best means of providing "needed protection and preservation" of big game. This ordinance would have created a dual licensing system whereby a hunter would pay 1,000 rupees for the right to shoot throughout Uganda or 500 rupees for a particular district. Moreover, only a specified number of species could be shot under each license: twelve elephants, three rhinoceroses, six hippopotamuses, one giraffe, and one buffalo. A further charge of 100 rupees was levied for each elephant actually bagged. Lastly, each sportsman was required to submit to the colonial authorities a list of all game killed. Government officials, caravan leaders shooting "for the pot," and farmers or plantation owners defending crops or property were exempted from this ordinance.

To assure additional protection for Uganda's elephants, Berkeley proposed to prohibit issuance of licenses to professional ivory hunters. He also suggested that the colonial administration give public notice to all African peoples that, six months after adoption of the ordinance, all tusks weighing ten pounds or less would be subject to confiscation. Finally, Berkeley recommended that the Foreign Office authorize Uganda's Commissioner to declare any district "closed" to hunting. He refused, however, to commit the colonial administration on the game sanctuary issue, claiming instead that "the matter would at present offer various and not inconsiderable difficulties. . .and it may therefore as well be left over for consideration at some future period."[3]

Although these proposals incorporated Salisbury's suggestions that the country's game laws be predicated upon bag limits and high license fees, the Foreign Office rejected Berkeley's plan without comment. It then imposed an ordinance on Uganda that failed to take local conditions into account. Under these regulations, a sport license cost 375 rupees,

---

2. Salisbury to Berkeley, 27 May 1896, FOCP 6849/175. As indicated in Chapter I, this communication also was dispatched to Sir Arthur Hardinge, Commissioner of Kenya.

3. Berkeley to Salisbury, 25 November 1896, Great Britain, *Correspondence Relating to the Preservation of Wild Animals in Africa*, Cd. 3189 (1906), pp. 31-4.

and a license for settlers and government officials cost 5 rupees. This enabled sportsmen and government officials to kill anything outside a game reserve except for two each of elephant (male), rhinoceros, hippopotamus, buffalo, and giraffe. These regulations authorized a Sub-Commissioner to remove the restriction if hunters paid 180 rupees for every additional elephant and 90 rupees for each extra rhinoceros, hippopotamus, buffalo, or giraffe killed. The settler's license allowed the bearer to hunt within his own district and kill only four animals per month of Thomson's gazelle, Grant's gazelle, hartebeest, impala, and wildebeest.[4]

By preserving rather than controlling the elephant and reducing the number of elephants that could be shot on license from twelve to two, the Foreign Office precipitated a population explosion which reached the critical stage in only twenty years. In the interim, the British government and colonial authorities exacerbated the problem by adopting policies that further stimulated the growth of Uganda's elephant population. Sir Harry Johnston—explorer, imperialist, big game hunter, and wildlife enthusiast—shaped many of these early programs. One month after becoming Uganda's Special Commissioner in October 1899, Johnston asked the Foreign Office for permission to proclaim a temporary game reserve in the Lake Rudolf region. About three months later, the Foreign Office approved this request and the colonial administration established the Sugota Game Reserve, an area which covered 13,000 square miles and included much of the Pokot and Turkana country.[5]

Johnston was concerned about the African hunter's effect on wildlife, particularly the elephant. Prior to 1900, Africans, armed with old-fashioned flintlocks, killed an untold number of elephants to supply the lucrative Arab-dominated ivory trade. According to Charles Pitman, who became Uganda's Game Warden in 1925, "armed natives [who] were sent ahead into various parts of Uganda to pave the way for British Administration" also helped reduce the elephant population to feed the ivory trade. Johnston believed that these two threats eventually would bring about the elephant's extinction in every district except Karamoja, an extremely dry and inaccessible area in north-eastern Uganda.[6]

To prevent Africans from hunting and slaughtering elephants, Johnston concluded an agreement with the Kingdom of Buganda that provided for a precise definition of its territorial boundaries and an abrogation of any rights of suzerainty, tribute, or privileged

---

4. FO to Ternan, 28 August 1899, Cd. 3189, p. 64.

5. G. Archer, *Personal and Historical Memoirs of an East African Administrator* (London: Oliver and Boyd, 1963), p. 144; FO to Johnston, 11 January 1900, FOCP 7404/12; Johnston to Salisbury, 21 November 1899, FOCP 7404/4. For further information about Johnston's life, see A. Johnston, *The Life and Letters of Sir Harry Johnston* (New York: Cape and Smith, 1929); Harry H. Johnston, *The Story of My Life* (Indianapolis: Bobbs Merrill, 1923); and Roland Oliver, *Harry Johnston and the Scramble for Africa* (New York: St. Martin's Press, 1957).

6. Archer, *Personal Memoirs*, pp. 2-3; C.R.S. Pitman, Elephant Control, Pitman Papers, Museum of Natural History Library, 289 FL #1, p. 38.

position over the Protectorate's adjoining provinces. Under the old system, African hunters had sallied forth several times a year and killed elephants in the Kingdoms of Toro, Ankole, and Bunyoro. In Buganda, Johnston induced the regents and chiefs to enact a law through the Lukiko, or council, which prohibited killing female or immature male elephants. As far as the country's other areas were concerned, Johnston simply banned the killing of elephants. He informed the Foreign Office, however, that this law would be a "dead letter" in many districts until the administration had acquired "a firmer hold over the country." Johnston also established a 2,500-square mile elephant reserve in Bunyoro and one of 200 square miles in Toro. Finally, he dispatched a "large force of police" to guard Sugota Game Reserve.[7]

Johnston's efforts to preserve Uganda's elephants succeeded to such an extent that Sir James Hayes Sadler, the country's Commissioner from 1902 to 1905, favored the adoption of a harsher game ordinance. Sadler claimed the change was necessary because complaints had been received from all over the Protectorate about the damage done to plantations and shambas by elephants. To prevent a resurgence of the ivory trade among African hunters, Sadler refused to permit the outright killing of elephants to protect agricultural settlements. He ordered local European administrators to advise any African whose shamba was being raided by elephants to scare the beasts away by lighting fires, shooting guns, or beating drums. When this failed to curtail shamba attacks, Sadler observed, "What we have to do is, first, to preserve the cultivation, secondly, to preserve the elephant which destroys the cultivation, [and] to find means by which both ends can be met." Sadler therefore issued a £10 hunting license to African chiefs in high risk regions, which authorized the shooting of two elephants. If an individual or community could not afford the fee, the amendment allowed the nearest chief "to shoot one, or at the most two elephants actually doing damage." The Foreign Office approved Sadler's scheme.[8]

Clearly, the success or failure of this policy depended on the colonial administration's ability to stop elephant attacks on African shambas. Unfortunately, this issue failed to attract the attention of the British government or the Fauna Preservation Society, probably because Uganda's Africans lacked the political organization necessary to express their grievances. Even when Edward Buxton led a deputation to the Colonial Office in 1905, to discuss wildlife preservation in East Africa, the elephant problem was not on the agenda.[9]

---

7. Johnston to Salisbury, 5 April 1900, FO 403/303.

8. Sadler to Lansdowne, 1 May 1903, FO 403/355; copy in FO 2/818. Also, see FO to Sadler, 16 June 1903, FO 403/355; copy in FO 2/818.

9. "Minutes of Proceedings at a Deputation From the Society for the Preservation of the Fauna of the Empire to the Right Hon. Alfred Lyttelton, His Majesty's Secretary for the Colonies," *Journal of the Society for the Preservation of the Wild Fauna of the Empire*, Vol. I (1905), pp. 11-2.

To correct this situation, Sadler submitted a report to the British government, reviewing the general state of game preservation until the end of 1905, and calling for a more realistic elephant policy. He dismissed the notion that the country's game reserves were only paper creations designed to calm public opinion in England, and pointed out that, since 1902, wildlife had increased and not a single species "was even remotely threatened with extinction." Sadler believed it was unnecessary to create an expensive policing system in the reserves as their sanctity already was "fully respected."

With regard to elephants, Sadler argued that in the Kingdoms of Toro, Ankole, and Bunyoro, their preservation was "a hardship to the people" and "a decided nuisance in the plantations." He maintained that in most places the African required more protection than the elephant. Sadler concluded his comments by reiterating Uganda's basic ecological dilemma—"how to preserve the elephant, and at the same time protect the cultivator whose crops he destroys."[10]

Six months after this report, Acting Commissioner O.A.J. Wilson advised the Colonial Office that the British government's philosophy of preserving Uganda's elephants at all costs placed African communities in an untenable position:

Maasai Warriors. The Maasai people have played a vital role in wildlife conservation efforts in Kenya and Tanzania.

Courtesy of the author

---

10. Sadler to Lyttelton, 1 November 1905, CO/536/3.

I know there is much that can be put forward in opposition to the absolute preservation of Game and I am inclined to believe that the movers in the policy having that object have not acquired a full grasp of all affecting circumstances. Otherwise, it would almost seem that a tenderness of feeling in this particular direction is allowed to obscure the senses to the happening of much actual distress in another and more serious direction. I have seen villages and plantations which had just been devastated by elephants— and worse, I have passed through districts where lives of the native have been lost and those remaining were in daily danger through the outrageous aggressions of these protected beasts.[11]

Lion with "danger beyond this point sign." Despite encroaching civilization, the lion remains an ever-present danger.

Courtesy of Gerald Rilling.

These protestations caused a policy reassessment in the British government and the Fauna Preservation Society. When Buxton led another deputation to the Colonial Office in 1906, Lord Curzon, representing the Fauna Preservation Society, suggested that the views of those people who protested against the existence of game reserves "on agricultural grounds, on economical grounds, on the grounds of protection for the natives, and on the grounds of the depredations alleged to be committed by the wild game" should be taken

11. Wilson to Elgin, 4 April 1906, CO 536/6.

into consideration by British policymakers. Unfortunately, the delegates failed to go beyond these generalities and Uganda's elephant problem remained troublesome.[12]

The colonial administration tried to resolve the matter by enacting a new game ordinance, which increased license fees to limit the number of big game hunters in Uganda. It also provided financial compensation for Africans whose crops were damaged or destroyed by elephants. Under this scheme, the government permitted chiefs to kill up to two marauding elephants without a license. An administration official then divided the ivory between the chief, the government, and the shamba owner, who also kept the carcasses.[13]

Despite these concessions, most Africans continued to resent the elephant and all game laws. In January 1908, Sir Hesketh Bell, Uganda's first governor, tried to reverse this situation by recommending that "no considerations connected either with sport or with the preservation of fauna should be allowed to weigh against the great hardships to which the natives of this country are now being subjected." As evidence, he pointed out that since 1905, elephants had killed or severely wounded 101 people in the Kingdoms of Toro and Buganda. Bell also deplored the fact that an African whose shamba was being ravaged by elephants was not allowed to shoot them:

> He can only send to his chief, who is empowered to act in such cases, and is advised, in the meantime, to try to frighten the animals off by shouting and beating drums. The chief may take two or three days to reach the spot, and by the time he arrives on the scene the elephants are probably thirty or forty miles off, and quite out of reach. The subject is one that bristles with difficulties, and. . .the animals are being protected to such a degree that they are devastating a populous and promising country.

Lastly, Bell observed that African complaints about this problem were "so strong and frequent that action can no longer be delayed."[14]

To avoid political trouble, the colonial administration enacted a policy later in 1908 to use professional elephant hunters to "thin out" huge herds. The special govern-

---

12. "Minutes of Proceedings at a Deputation From the Society for the Preservation of the Wild Fauna of the Empire to the Right Hon. The Earl of Elgin, His Majesty's Secretary of State for the Colonies," *Journal of the Society for the Preservation of the Wild Fauna of the Empire*, Vol. II (1906), p. 23. The fact that the local administration enjoyed such wide discretionary powers alarmed Sir Hesketh Bell, Uganda's first governor. In his memoirs, Bell claimed that "my responsibilities are great. Mistakes that I may make have consequences of untold importance in the future. Unlike the case of my other colonial administrators, I have no Legislature to share my responsibility or limit my power." H. Bell, *Glimpses of a Governor's Life* (London: Sampson Lowe, Marston and Company Ltd., 1946), p. 96.

13. Bell to Elgin, 17 November 1906, Great Britain, *Further Correspondence Relating to the Preservation of Wild Animals in Africa*, Cd. 4472 (1909), p. 41.

14. Bell to Elgin, 21 January 1908, CO 536/18; Bell to Crewe, 22 April 1909, Great Britain, *Further Correspondence Relating to the Preservation of Wild Animals in Africa*, Cd. 5136 (1910), p. 44.

ment licenses purchased by these hunters entitled them to shoot ten or twenty elephants and keep 50 percent of the ivory, the remainder to be turned over to colonial authorities. According to G.H. Anderson, a noted big game hunter, this scheme caused all the old Kenya and Uganda elephant hunters to come out of retirement "like a swarm of bees around a honey-pot." Many killed only bulls carrying heavy tusks and ignored the real shamba raiders, usually females or young males. The colonial administration abandoned this strategy and discontinued efforts to control the marauding beasts.[15]

By November 1909, economic difficulties forced Alexander Boyle, Uganda's Acting Governor, to adopt a policy which further increased the elephant population. His decision stemmed from the fact that the British government's grant-in-aid to Uganda had increased from £85,000 in 1907-1908 to £103,262 in 1909-1910. To help reduce the country's dependence on the British taxpayer, Boyle proposed to amend the 1906 Game Ordinance by requiring European sportsmen to purchase a special elephant license, costing from 150 to 450 rupees. On 5 April 1910, the Colonial Office approved this recommendation and unwittingly sacrificed African interests for increased revenues. The following figures show how drastically government earnings from game licenses dropped because of Boyle's plan. [16]

TABLE II			
REVENUE FROM GAME LICENCES			
1907-8	£2,391	1910-11	(to the end of November) £1,450
1908-9	£3,329		
1909-10	£3,872	1911-12	(estimated) £2,100

There also was a noticeable reduction in the number of big game hunters operating in Uganda. The colonial administration believed many of them went to Kenya where there was a "wider selection of game" and less expensive licensing fees. According to Stanley Tomkins, who had served for a time as Acting Governor, this exodus enabled the country's elephants to become "still more dangerous and destructive [and] bolder in approaching inhabited areas." Faced with increased herds and decreased revenues, the British government acceded to Tomkins's request to abolish the 1906 Game Ordinance amendment.[17]

15. G.H. Anderson, *African Safaris* (Nakuru: Nakuru Press, c. 1946), p. 101; also, see B. Kinloch, *The Shamba Raiders* (London: Collins and Harvill Press, 1972), p. 112.

16. H.B. Thomas and R. Scott, *Uganda* (London: Oxford University Press, 1935), p. 504; Boyle to Crewe, 22 November 1909, Cd. 5136, pp. 71-2; Crewe to Boyle, 5 April 1910, Cd. 5136, p. 104; Tomkins to Harcourt, 10 February 1911, Great Britain, *Further Correspondence Relating to the Preservation of Wild Animals*, Cd. 5775 (1911), p. 25; Harcourt to Jackson, 7 April 1911, Cd. 5775, p. 30.

17. R.M.A. Van Zwanenberg with Anne King, *An Economic History of Kenya and Uganda 1800-1970* (London: Macmillan Press Ltd., 1977), pp. 62-3.

In retrospect, it seems incredible that the colonial administration remained committed to elephant preservation, especially in view of the fact that African peasants usually produced about 8 percent of Uganda's exports. Yet, as late as 1913, Sir Frederick Jackson, Governor of Uganda, argued in favor of an international agreement to protect the country's elephants. In the face of serious and widespread shamba raids, the colonial administration gradually adopted a more realistic elephant control policy.[18]

From 1917 to 1921, authorities issued more than 20,000 rounds of ammunition to African hunters; and, from 1918 onward, District Commissioners enlisted European elephant hunters to thin the herds. As payment, the colonial administration allowed hunters to keep a percentage of the ivory. Although this scheme resulted in the destruction of approximately 4,000 elephants between 1917 and 1921, it failed to achieve meaningful long-term results, largely because most hunters again shot only bulls with heavy ivory.[19]

Other hunters, hoping to make easy money, resorted to elaborate subterfuges to justify killing innocent elephants. According to Keith Caldwell, a conservationist with wide East African experience, when a "certain European" discovered that elephants no longer were doing damage in his district, he paid an African to dig up roots in a shamba and stamp the ground with stuffed elephant feet. After the District Commissioner investigated this "attack," he permitted the European to shoot two elephants per day until the beasts retreated.[20]

Another factor that contributed to this plan's collapse concerned the escapades of unskilled African hunters who wounded numerous elephants, only to have the half-crazed beasts terrorize scores of villages. Like their European counterparts, Africans often ignored shamba raiders and concentrated on the big tuskers. According to Charles Swynnerton, a Tanganyika Game Department official who studied Uganda's elephant problem, this practice actually increased the pressure on the country's African farmers:

> Shooting of this type broke up the herds, the migrations and the feeding habits of the elephants, and these, always moved greatly when much shot at and now harried from pillar to post, and getting no time for their ordinary leisured feeding, turned to the shambas as the means of readiest sustenance.[21]

---

18. Jackson to Harcourt, 18 October 1913, CO 885/22.

19. K. Kittenberger, *Big Game Hunting and Collecting in East Africa 1903-1926* (London: Edward Arnold, 1929), p. 89; Kinloch, *Shamba Raiders*, pp. 111-2; Pitman, Elephant Control, p. 33; Uganda Protectorate, *Report on the Control of Elephants in Uganda* (Entebbe: The Government Press, 1923), p.11; enclosure in Archer to Thomas, 17 March 1924, CO 536/130.

20. K. Caldwell, "The Commercialisation of Game," *Journal of the Society for the Preservation of the Fauna of the Empire*, New Series Part VII (1927), p. 85.

21. *Report on the Control of Elephants in Uganda*, pp. 11-2; Eliot to Churchill, 5 July 1922, CO 536/119.

In view of these shortcomings, Acting Governor E.C. Eliot convened a committee to investigate the matter and make recommendations as to the best means of resolving the issue. The committee, under the chairmanship of P.W. Cooper, Provincial Commissioner of Western Province, met in March 1922, to review Uganda's wildlife policy. It drew attention "to the spasmodic and indefinite character" of the protective measures used during the 1917-1921 period, and pointed out that "there are more elephants in Uganda at present than ever before."[22]

The Cooper committee favored the adoption of a three-step program wherein Uganda would be divided into elephant and non-elephant regions, and specially assembled teams, financed by the government, would drive all the beasts into the latter zone. Malingering or belligerent animals would be killed. Any elephant that returned to a restricted area would be regarded as vermin and shot, with the ivory shared between the colonial administration and the hunter.[23] However, E.B. Harvis, Deputy to the Governor, rejected these proposals as being "financially impracticable."[24]

When Uganda's Executive Council met on 8 December 1922, it approved an alternate plan, formulated by Eliot, whereby the government issued special licenses to "approved hunters," enabling them to shoot up to twenty elephants. To induce them to kill females and young males, the real culprits, Eliot drew up an escalating payment schedule awarding up to 150 shillings for heavy (viz. bull) tusks.[25]

On 12 February 1923, Sir Geoffrey Archer, a nephew of Sir Frederick Jackson and a naturalist and sportsman in his own right, arrived in Entebbe to become governor. Archer branded the Eliot plan a "ghastly mistake" and refused to authorize the issuance of special hunting licenses. Archer justified his position by saying:

> Professional hunters would not concern themselves with protecting shambas. . .but would establish themselves, each and all, in the main haunts of the elephants throughout the Protectorate. As one herd was stampeded by riflefire, it would arrive in a new locality only to be fired at again by another hunter, or party of hunters working together. And in the end we should have the whole of the elephant population in Uganda terrified and crashing its way across country and doing no end of damage in the course of a precipitate flight from pillar to post.[26]

---

22. Eliot to Churchill, 5 July 1922, and enclosure.

23. *Ibid.*

24. *Report on the Control of Elephants in Uganda*, p. 121; Archer to Devonshire, 30 April 1923, CO 536/125.

25. Executive Council Minutes, 8 December 1922, CO 685/8. A notice of Eliot's plan dated 16 December 1922 is contained in CO 536/124; a copy also is in the *Uganda Official Gazette*, 30 December 1922. In his *Personal Memoirs*, p. 145, Archer mistakenly says the license entitled each hunter to shoot thirty elephants.

26. Archer, *Personal Memoirs*, p. 146.

Privately, however, he doubted whether Uganda's Executive Council—comprised of the Chief Secretary, Treasurer, Attorney-General, Principal Medical Officer, and several other office-bound administrators—would have "any particular vision or useful idea as to how best to control masses of wild animals.[27]

Archer's solution to the elephant dilemma was to eliminate the profit motive from elephant control. Instead of paying hunters according to ivory weight, he wanted to hire two full-time control officers—one for Toro and the other for Bunyoro—on an annual fixed salary of £600 plus traveling expenses. As far as Buganda was concerned, Archer believed that, because of the growing herds, "the necessity of exterminating the elephants in that Province might have to be faced." Additionally, he suggested that the colonial administration engage the services of Charles Swynnerton, Tanganyika's Game Warden, to supervise the operation.[28]

When the Executive Council considered Archer's plan, Attorney-General A. Hogg observed that the men employed to kill elephants might also engage in cross border ivory smuggling. He recommended that their compensation be a salary plus a fixed reward for each elephant killed. Archer said the smuggling issue could be resolved by granting a percentage of the ivory's value to the *Lukiko* (cabinet). He maintained this would give all chiefs an interest in reporting the activities of government hunters.

After this exchange, the Executive Council adopted a new strategy and agreed to employ five temporary full-time European hunters on a fixed salary of 1,000 shillings per month. Archer wanted the three additional hunters posted to Masaka District, Mubendi District, and Bulemezi and Buruli counties, all located in the Kingdom of Buganda. The Executive Council postponed implementation of the plan until Swynnerton's arrival.[29]

Archer further elaborated on this scheme in a dispatch to the Colonial Office. Like Sir James Hayes Sadler, Archer believed that the colonial government's primary responsibility was to provide "adequate protection of cultivation" in African areas and to ensure the continued existence of at least some of Uganda's elephants. Archer believed that it was logistically impossible to safeguard crops in the country's interior. Thus, he suggested that "the inhabitants of those areas should be induced to move to the settled and closely cultivated districts where they can be given protection and can, at the same time, be brought under better administrative control."

On elephant preservation, Archer maintained that "there must be no conflict in the hunter's mind of financial gain versus an adequate discharge of duty." By employing

---

27. *Ibid.*

28. *Ibid.*; Executive Council Minutes, 6 April 1923, CO 685/8.

29. Executive Council Minutes, 6 April 1923.

fixed-wage hunters, he thought it would be financially immaterial whether two elephants or twenty were shot. He ended his report by pointing out:

> If, eventually certain herds of elephants in thickly populated and cultivated areas were found impossible to control and impossible to move forward into an area where they could do no harm, there will then be no alternative but to exterminate them.[30]

Unfortunately, by April 1923, dozens of professional European elephant hunters already had arrived in Kampala from all over Africa—particularly South Africa and Kenya—hoping to participate in Eliot's percentage plan. When the hunters learned of Archer's scheme they charged that they had been "misled and ruined" by the colonial administration's premature announcement in the *Uganda Gazette* of the special license project, and demanded an interview with the Governor.

Archer consented, and, when a deputation arrived at Government House, he spoke to them "frankly as one hunter to another." Archer said they knew as well as he that Eliot's idea was a prescription for disaster. Captain Roy Salmon admitted that the scheme "was the elephant hunters' dream come true." According to Archer, men like Salmon "stood to make very easily in the course of a few months several thousands of pounds after paying all expenses." Under the circumstances, however, Archer offered to see to it that the hunters suffered "no financial loss" getting to and from Uganda. The meeting therefore adjourned in a relatively amiable atmosphere.[31]

On 25 September 1923, Charles Swynnerton arrived in Entebbe "to render advice as to the control of elephants." After visiting Masindi and Fort Portal, Swynnerton proceeded to the tiny government hill station at Mubende in the Kingdom of Buganda to participate in a conference between Archer and several professional hunters, including Pete Pearson and Captain Salmon. After discussing all aspects of the elephant problem, the conferees formed a six-man Elephant Control Staff to study and plot the movements of the country's herds. The staff then would divide Uganda into six zones, print maps, and telegraph herd movements from one control officer to another so the elephants could be driven back into less populated areas. The conferees hoped this would stop seasonal elephant migrations into cultivated regions and justify the destruction of all shamba raiders. To prevent financial speculation or unnecessary shooting, all ivory automatically would go to the government.

Swynnerton submitted his report to the authorities on 6 November 1923. To help explain the reason for Uganda's burgeoning elephant herds, he solicited the views of the

---

30. Archer to Devonshire, 30 April 1923, CO 536/125.

31. Archer, *Personal Memoirs*, pp. 146-7.

Katikiro, or Prime Minister, of Buganda, Sir Apolo Kagwa, a man whose country had suffered tremendously from the ravages of these beasts. According to Kagwa:

> Before the Europeans came the elephants were far less troublesome because, firstly, the population was more concentrated, secondly, the elephants were hunted down remorselessly when they appeared near cultivation.[32]

As the religious wars of the late 1880s scattered the human population of Buganda and neighboring territories and the colonial administration enacted wildlife preservation laws, elephant herds grew at an alarming rate. Indeed, Swynnerton warned the government that Uganda's elephants—which he estimated to be somewhere under 30,000—would double in the next thirty years, despite the fact that 1,000 would be killed annually by man and one half the yearly progeny would be lost to natural causes.

To prevent Uganda from being taken over by herds of hungry elephants, Swynnerton suggested that the country be divided into cultivated zones, especially selected and protected from elephants; elephant reserves in which all hunting would be prohibited; and buffer areas in which licensed shooting would be allowed. On 17 March 1924, Governor Archer informed the Colonial Office that Swynnerton's report was "in complete agreement with the views I have formed." In addition, he said that, for the present, four salaried European hunters—to be known as Game Rangers—were sufficient to control Uganda's marauding elephants. Archer also believed that the appointment of a full-time Game Warden was "a most urgent necessity."[33] Within three months, Archer hired the Game Rangers—Captain Roy Salmon, F.G. Banks, P.C. Pearson, and Captain C.D.K. Palmer Kerrison—and approved the use of trained African hunters to work with each of them.[34]

Thus, by the middle of 1924, Archer had laid the foundation of Uganda's Game Department. In December, Keith Caldwell, then Kenya's Deputy Game Warden, arrived in Entebbe to organize the Department's administration. Unfortunately, he was recalled after three weeks for duty with the Royal Safari of the Duke and Duchess of York. Although Archer appointed Charles Pitman—an experienced big game hunter and knowledgeable naturalist—to the post of Acting Game Warden, Caldwell's departure restricted the Department's operations for four months.[35]

---

32. *Ibid.*, pp. 163-4; *Report on the Control of Elephants in Uganda*, p. 3.

33. *Report on the Control of Elephants in Uganda*, p. 9.

34. Archer to Thomas, 17 March 1924, CO 536/130.

35. *Annual Report Game Department 1925*, p. 5.

The Game Department finally came into being on 26 September 1925, when Caldwell returned to Uganda and turned over the office of Game Warden to Pitman. By this time, the wildlife situation was at the crisis stage, with "nearly 75 percent of Uganda. . .occupied by elephants." Unfortunately, public and private opinion hampered Pitman's efforts to resolve this issue by treating the Game Department as a Cinderella operation. Indeed, as late as June 1931, the *Uganda News* published an article declaring that "The starting of 'stunt' departments has been the greatest scandal in Uganda in recent years. Game Rangers where there is no game!" The colonial administration further hindered Pitman by requiring annual justification that the Game Department "was not a drain on the exchequer but, on the contrary, more than paid its way through the revenue obtained from the sale of control ivory and hunting licenses."[36]

Since Governor Archer and his successors already had determined that the only way to prevent elephants from raiding African shambas and European plantations was to kill them, Pitman was perforce committed to a massive extermination campaign.

Privately, however, Pitman questioned this strategy's long-term effectiveness:

> In 'control' operations elephants can be satisfactorily harried only to a limited extent. Once this limit is exceeded 'control' will defeat its object by dispersing herds, often scattering them far and wide, to exert increasing pressure on cultivation and settlement hitherto free from depredation. At the same time there could be no deviation from the avowed object of 'control' to protect the lives and property of the local inhabitants.[37]

Because of these reservations, Pitman initially attempted to implement a modified version of the Archer scheme to preserve as much wildlife as possible. Accordingly, when elephants attacked a shamba or plantation, a control officer would shoot one and, if the herd moved away, leave the rest alone. This tactic repeatedly failed because the elephants, or possibly another herd, returned to resume feeding. Reluctantly, Pitman decided to deal with elephants "in drastic fashion."[38]

Henceforth, the Game Department tried to confine herds to traditional breeding grounds or uninhabited areas where they could roam freely. Elephants found in other parts of the country were shot on sight. Pitman hoped this would prevent elephant encroachment on settled areas. In his first annual report, he noted that these "defensive fronts" varied according to local circumstances. In Bunyoro, for example, the front measured

---

36. Kinloch, *Shamba Raiders*, p. 113, 207; C.R.S. Pitman, Elephant Control: Ten Years On, Pitman Papers, Museum of Natural History Library, Z89 FP #3.

37. Pitman, Elephant Control: Ten Years On, p. 1.

38. *Ibid.*, p. 14; *Annual Report Game Department 1925*, p. 14.

150 miles, while in Toro, where there were several small breeding grounds, a series of mini fronts contained the elephants.[39]

Initially, this plan appeared to be a success. At the June 1925 Provincial Commissioner's Conference, the delegates expressed their appreciation to the authorities for creating a Game Department and adopting an elephant control policy. By the end of the year, Pitman divulged that his staff had killed 587 elephants and that:

> From all districts where the Game Rangers and their staffs have been operating reports have testified to the success of the methods employed, and a decided check has been put on shamba destruction.[40]

Again in 1927, the Department claimed that reports from all control areas indicated "a diminution of damage done by elephants and a falling off in the number of complaints."[41]

Notwithstanding the Game Department's optimism, the defensive front strategy ultimately failed to control or prevent elephant raids on shambas and plantations. In Toro District, impenetrable swamps and dense elephant grass, often fifteen to twenty feet tall, formed ideal covers for elephant herds. After the colonial administration started paying Toro's European planters £8 for each twenty elephants shot, F.G. Banks, the region's Game Ranger, still maintained that "herds were increasing and that the killing had to be accelerated." Even when the Game Department authorized Banks to encourage his African staff to attack elephants on "every possible occasion," the Toro herds continued to increase.[42]

To bring the situation under control, the Game Department devised the "Toro Special Elephant Scheme," which licensed six European hunters for six months to shoot up to 100 elephants each. Although by mid-April 1933, these hunters had succeeded in shooting more than four hundred shamba raiders, Banks remained pessimistic. In his official report, he noted that while some herds had been reduced, the scheme's general impact was "scarcely noticeable." In 1934, even the Game Department admitted:

> In spite of heavy elephant shooting and some consequent reduction during the last twelve years or more, elephants are still too plentiful in Toro where they have good protection in the numerous swamps and dense jungles.[43]

---

39. *Annual Report Game Department 1925*, p. 13.

40. *Ibid.*, p. 14.

41. Uganda Protectorate, *Annual Report Game Department 1927* (Entebbe: The Government Printer, 1928), p. 8.

42. Scott to Amery, 10 September 1928, CO 536/150; Amery to Gowers, 13 December 1928, CO 536/150; Uganda Protectorate, *Annual Report Game Department 1931* (Entebbe: The Government Printer, 1935), p. 20.

43. *Annual Report Game Department 1932*, p. 5; Uganda Protectorate, *Annual Report Game Department 1933* (Entebbe: The Government Printer, 1934), p. 10; Uganda Protectorate, *Annual Report Game Department 1934* (Entebbe: The Government Printer), p. 20.

On a nationwide scale circumstances were equally disappointing. In 1935, Pitman revealed that, with the exception of the Eastern Province, control measures were still necessary in nearly every district, despite the fact that the Department had killed about 14,000 elephants during the past decade. The following year, he wearily observed that for every elephant shot it seemed as if two appeared as replacements. By 1937, a defeated Pitman declared, "The outstanding feature of the elephant situation is the abundance of elephants." [44]

To make matters worse, inadequate government financing continued to hamper the Department's operations. Pitman therefore had to use European officers of the King's African Rifles 4th Battalion in many control operations. At times, even European administrative officials helped by filling in as temporary Game Rangers. Throughout the 1930s, for example, Rennie Bere, then an Assistant District Commissioner, claimed he rarely missed an opportunity to shoot marauding elephants.[45]

Personnel shortages also plagued the Game Department. Rinderpest control operations frequently forced Pitman to relieve African Game Guards from their normal duties to kill cattle and wild animals suspected of carrying the disease. In addition, an economic recession compelled the colonial administration to reduce the Department's staff to one European field officer and fifteen African Game Guards. Consequently by late 1949, in a country the size of the British Isles, there was a total field force of only two permanent European Game Rangers, forty-four African Game Guards, eight African Game Scouts, and seven African gun bearers.[46]

Another factor that prevented Pitman from resolving the elephant problem was the proliferation of game reserves from two in 1900 to five in 1935. They included Bunyoro and Gulu (1,800 square miles); Toro (200 square miles); Lake George (266 square miles); Lake Edward (216 square miles); and Damba (twelve square miles). Although these sanctuaries helped ensure the failure of the elephant control scheme, Pitman continued trying to preserve wildlife and to control the country's elephants until well after the end of the Second World War.

The growth of a small but profitable tourist industry prevented the abolition or alteration of these reserves. The most popular attraction was the Uganda Railway's fortnightly game viewing excursions to Murchison Falls via the luxurious river steamer

---

44. Uganda Protectorate, *Annual Report Game Department 1935* (Entebbe: The Government Printer, 1936), p. 8; Uganda Protectorate, *Annual Report Game Department 1936* (Entebbe: The Government Printer, 1937), p. 9; Uganda Protectorate, *Annual Report Game Department 1937* (Entebbe: The Government Printer, 1938), p. 9.

45. Pitman, Elephant Control: Ten Years On, p. 17; *Annual Report Game Department 1927*, p. 10; R. Bere, A Spear for the Rhinoceros, unpublished manuscript in author's possession, p. 91.

46. Uganda Protectorate, *Annual Report Game Department 1929* (Entebbe: The Government Printer, 1930), p. 11; *Annual Report Game Department 1932*, p.4; Kinloch, *Shamba Raiders*, p. 104.

S. W. Lugard. According to Pitman, these trips caused tremendous excitement and interest in Uganda's wildlife:

> The river is entered at such an hour as to make the journey to the Falls (approximately thirty miles as the stream winds) by daylight, and immediately as one leaves [Lake Kyoga] the pageant of nature begins. . .Elephants are nearly always feeding amongst the islands. . .About two hours later the head of the delta is reached; here the mainstream is entered and one's advent is welcomed by a couple of hundred of hippopotami. . .Thence onwards excitement increases to fever pitch: elephants swarm on either side; hippopotami become more and more numerous; crocodiles in hundreds fringe the banks. . .and various antelopes. . .feed in leisurely fashion. Baboons with rancous bark. . .voice their resentment at the intrusion of their domain, while timid. . .colobus monkeys are seen on either bank. . .In the earlier hours. . .both buffaloes and lions have been observed from the steamer.[47]

Apart from the revenues these excursions generated, the colonial treasury earned income from the sale of hunting licenses. From 1925 to 1935, this amount totalled £43,741, a welcome sum for the financially starved administration. The continued presence of big game hunters obviously depended on the existence of large herds of wild animals, including elephants; and the only way to guarantee their future preservation was by the maintenance of extensive game reserves. So, unable to abandon either game reserves or elephant control, the colonial administration pursued both programs until the post-1945 period.

According to Alistair Graham, a noted ecologist and former warden of the Kenya Game Department, Uganda's elephant problem stemmed not so much from policy inconsistency as from a gross lack of scientific expertise. Between 1924 and 1939, for example, half the country's Game Rangers "sported military rank" and possessed little or no scientific training. As a result, control operations were organized "along the lines of a military campaign" without the slightest reference to ecological principles. Graham also accused Pitman and his staff of viewing elephants as nothing more than a "horde of hostile barbarians" to be destroyed wherever and whenever they attacked human settlements.[48]

More importantly, Graham maintained that Pitman misunderstood the nature of Uganda's elephant dilemma. He believed that Pitman and Swynnerton had failed to appreciate the true size of the country's herds. They based their calculations on guesses "arrived at by driving about from place to place for a while, judging what they saw of the elephants

---

47. C.R.S. Pitman, *A Game Warden Among His Charges* (London: Nisbet, 1931, pp. 281-2; *Annual Report Game Department 1929*, p. 7. Also, see C.R.S. Pitman, *A Game Warden Takes Stock* (London: Nisbet, 1942).

48. A. Graham, *The Gardeners of Eden* (London: George Allen and Unwin Ltd., 1973), pp. 98-9.

according to whether they thought them 'a lot' or 'a few.'" Swynnerton reckoned there were about 30,000 in Uganda, while Pitman believed there were approximately 20,000; the actual figure, Graham claims, was closer to 50,000.[49]

Consequently, as an expanding human population squeezed the elephants into smaller and smaller areas, Pitman presumed that the control scheme was ineffective because the herds appeared to be increasing. He therefore ordered the destruction of more elephants at a time when herds were dangerously low. Graham contended that Pitman's actions reduced the elephant's range from 75 percent in 1924, to less than 13 percent in 1973.[50]

Although Graham's analysis was unpopular with many former Game Department officials, his theories gained a degree of acceptance throughout East Africa, possibly because they could be used as further evidence to condemn the British colonial rule. Nevertheless, Graham all but ignores the reality of day-to-day life in colonial Uganda. The fact that so many Game Department officials had military backgrounds, and lacked scientific training indicates more than an administrative inadequacy. Living conditions throughout East Africa were often harsh and transportation facilities were, for the most part, non-existent. Living in the field obviously required individuals who possessed considerable physical strength and stamina. Military men were a natural, perhaps necessary choice. Low pay and poor advancement opportunities also prevented many university graduates from joining one of East Africa's Game Departments. Thus, it is surprising that men like Ritchie and Swynnerton, both with university training, devoted their careers to wildlife preservation.[51]

With regard to Graham's allegation that Pitman and Swynnerton failed to calculate the size of Uganda's elephant herds properly—thereby precipitating their destruction—it must be remembered that staffing shortages and inadequate transportation made it impossible to conduct an accurate census. As late as 1965-1966, R.M. Laws, I.S.C. Parker, and R.C.B. Johnstone—all of whom conducted research for the Nuffield Unit of Tropical Animal Ecology in North Bunyoro—experienced difficulty in counting Uganda's elephants. After more than a hundred routine observation flights and three complete aerial surveys, they reported mathematical errors of up to 27.9 percent.[52]

The same can be said of the accusation that the Game Department unnecessarily hunted the country's elephants to the brink of extinction. As long as animals raided shambas and plantations, Pitman was forced to shoot them. To have done otherwise would have

---

49. *Ibid.*, p. 95.

50. *Ibid.*, p. 95.

51. Kinloch, *Shamba Raiders*, p. 212.

52. Laws, Parker, Johnstone, *Elephants and Their Habitat*, p. 65, 83.

caused an unacceptable man-animal conflict for Uganda's African and European communities. Indeed, it was this realization that convinced Pitman as well as Ritchie that national parks were needed to ensure the survival of East Africa's fauna.

Sir Geoffrey Archer, governor of Uganda from 1922 to 1924, played a vital role in the protectorate's so-called elephant control scheme.

Reproduced by permission of the Durham University Library (SAD 247/8/22).

Sir Harry Johnston was one of East Africa's earliest advocates of game preservation.

Courtesy of the Royal Commonwealth Society

C.R.S. Pitman served as Uganda's Game Warden from 1925 to 1950. He also was President of the Uganda Society from 1940 to 1941.

Uganda Society, Kampala; courtesy of Kraig Adler.

Graham's belief in science's ability to solve complex ecological problems also requires examination. Although science contributed significantly to the cause of wildlife preservation, history demonstrates that it has not been a panacea. In Tanganyika, for example, Swynnerton worked for years to demonstrate that the systematic extermination of wild animals would not stop the spread of sleeping sickness. Using all the scientific knowledge at his disposal, he eventually succeeded and saved countless thousands of innocent beasts from destruction. But, as will be shown in the next chapter, science also failed to establish a harmonious relationship between man and animal.

In summary, the 1895-1939 period in Uganda was a time of experimentation for the colonial administration and the Game Department. Unfortunately, all attempts to implement an ecologically sound and politically acceptable wildlife preservation policy failed, causing many to demand the eradication of the country's elephants. Pitman countered this argument by supporting the national park concept, which theoretically was supposed to create an atmosphere where man and animal could co-exist peacefully. Subsequent events would fail to justify Pitman's faith in the ability of national parks to resolve Uganda's elephant problem.

CHAPTER III

The Tsetse Fly and
Wildlife Preservation in Tanganyika

Unlike the ecological situation in Kenya and Uganda, where wildlife battled man for control of the land and its resources, Tanganyika (Tanzania) presented a more complex problem. A harmless-looking insect, the tsetse fly, was the focal point of a dilemma involving man, wild and domesticated animals, and parasitic flagellate protozoans called trypanosomes. According to some early scientific theories, wild animals facilitated the spread of deadly diseases—which emanated from the tsetse fly—to man and his domestic stock. Many European and African cattle owners demanded the eradication of the country's fauna for the sake of economic development. A small group of wildlife enthusiasts, led by Charles Swynnerton, Tanganyika's Game Warden, resisted this pressure and eventually proved that killing wild animals would not prevent the blood-sucking tsetse fly from carrying diseases to other living things.

Tanganyika's tsetse fly menace revolved around eight species: *G. Morsitans*, *G. Swynnertoni*, *G. Pallidipes*, *G. Austeni*, *G. Palpalis*, *G. Brevipalpis*, *G. Fiscipleuris*, and *G. Longpennis*. When any of these flies fed on a host with trypanosomes—normally a wild mammal—they often became infected and then transmitted the organism to man or beast. Two trypanosomes species—T. *Gambiense* and T. *Rhodesiense*—cause trypanosomiases, or sleeping sickness, while three others—T. *Brucei*, T. *Vivax*, and T. *Congolese*—are responsible for the horse and cattle disease known as nagana.

Sleeping sickness develops slowly, beginning with an inflammation at the site of the tsetse bite. For the next two years, the victim may experience a variety of symptoms, including headaches, fever, insomnia, daytime drowsiness, irregular body rashes, muscular cramps, swollen glands, and neurological pains. The patient then usually suffers from a fever and fast pulse rate accompanied by sweating, especially at night. Insomnia and daytime drowsiness also increase, and then malnutrition ensues because sleeplessness becomes so overpowering that the victim stops eating. General health steadily disintegrates until the patient becomes comatose and dies.[1] Fatality rates during the early colonial period

---

1. J.J. McKelvey, *Man against Tsetse: Struggle for Africa* (Ithaca: Cornell University Press, 1973), pp. 3-4.

were frighteningly high. In Uganda's Busoga Province, for example, about 200,000 people, approximately two-thirds of the population, died as a result of the 1902-1905 epidemic.[2]

In its most acute form, nagana strikes more quickly than sleeping sickness and causes animal deaths within weeks. According to V.S. Leese, a veterinarian with East African experience, cows were particularly susceptible and developed the following symptoms shortly after a tsetse attack:

> He grazes poorly, fitfully, or not at all; but may eat rations well. His flanks fall in, the head and neck droop a little, he stands about listlessly and a slight watery discharge runs from the eyes. . .Temperature generally [runs] between 98.5 and 103F in the morning and 102 to 106F in the evening. Cows in calf as a rule abort, or if in milk, go dry. There is frequently nothing very definite beyond the symptoms of fever. . .The end is often hastened by complications such as broncho-pneumonia or oedema of the lungs, or death may occur suddenly in the night or on the march.[3]

Although the lack of reliable records made it difficult to determine the fatality rate that occurred among domestic stock, T.A.M. Nash, former Director of the West African Institute for Trypanosomiasis Research in Kaduna, Nigeria, claimed that nagana was responsible for the death of "hundreds of thousands of domestic animals."[4] For Tanganyika, where so many people were engaged in pastoral pursuits, the presence of this disease had catastrophic political, social, and economic implications.

In the Kimbu country of western Tanganyika, for example, the tsetse fly made it "virtually impossible to keep any livestock other than a few chickens and doves." This not only isolated the Kimbu from neighboring communities but also prevented them from starting farms of their own. They gradually divided into smaller and smaller villages to survive. This in turn contributed to the general proliferation of loosely federated, quasi-independent chiefdoms, many of which were politically impotent and militarily weak.[5]

In other regions, the disease's impact was even more serious. Throughout the nineteenth century, central Tanganyika enjoyed an abundance of cattle, and "flesh, milk, eggs, and vegetables of every variety". By 1911, however, when Dr. Kurt Wohfel, a German veterinary bacteriologist, toured the area, nagana had ravaged the herds:

---

2. T.A.M. Nash, *Africa's Bane: The Tsetse Fly* (London: Collins, 1969), p. 32.

3 Quoted in T.S. Thomas, *Jubaland and the Northern Frontier District* (Nairobi: Uganda Railway Press, 1917), p. 159.

4. Nash, *Africa's Bane*, p. 17.

5. A. Shorter, *Chiefship in Western Tanzania: A Poltiical History of Kimbu* (Oxford: Clarendon Press, 1972), p. 67.

Over half of the Tabora District is overgrown with bush and forest. Glossina Morsitans are found throughout the area and cattle-keeping is possible only in limited areas of the district. At present, the entire western part is unsuited for cattle. With few exceptions, the situation is similar in the south. . .Already, some cattle are grazing in the tsetse-infested bush. This practice causes losses through nagana and prevents the herds from reaching their previous size. Today, there are only around 2,500 cattle left in the northwestern part of Tabora.[6]

Interestingly, some early European explorers and administrators reported that several African communities possessed a rudimentary knowledge of entomology. In 1865, Sir John Kirk pointed out that many pastoral peoples had experimented with a strange but apparently effective repellent:

> The fly avoids human excrement, so the natives told us, and we have found it true, and they say that cattle have been passed by day through fly country when smeared with a composition containing this. Native doctors have an herb to which they attribute a similar effect.[7]

David and Charles Livingstone revealed how Africans also used herbal medicines to ward off nagana:

> Moyara showed us a plant. . .and likewise told us how the medicine was prepared; the bark of the root, and what might please our homeopathic friends, a dozen of the tsetse are dried, and ground together into a fine powder. This mixture is administered internally; and the cattle are fumigated by burning under them the rest of the plant collected.[8]

Other Africans believed the destruction of disease-carrying wildlife was the most effective way of dealing with the tsetse fly. The eradication scheme used in the 1860s by Mzila, a Ngoni chief in northern Mozambique was a typical example:

> Drives with nets were organized across the country, and game, pigs and baboons were thus killed wholesale. If a herd of buffaloes was reported. . . it was at once hunted; if pigs appeared in a garden, they were at once traced down to their retreat and, the people round having been called out, were surrounded and killed.[9]

---

6. J.H. Speke, *What Led to the Discovery of the Source of the Nile* (London: Blackwood, 1864), p. 280.

7. K. Wofel, "Beitrage Zur Kenntnis Der Tsetse und Der Trypanosomiasis," *Der Pflanzer*, Vol. VII (1911), pp. 77-8. Quoted in H. Kjekshus, Ecology Control and Economic Development in East African History (London: Heinemann, 1977), p. 63.

8. J. Kirk, "On the Tsetse Fly of Tropical Africa," *The Journal of the Linnean Society*, Vol. VIII (1865), p. 154.

9. D. and C. Livingstone, *Narrative of an Expedition to the Zambezi and Its Tributaries* (London: John Murray, 1865), p. 233.

Thus, by employing one or a combination of these techniques, many of Tanganyika's indigenous communities achieved a tenuous stand-off with the forces of nature long before the advent of European colonialism in the latter half of the nineteenth century.

The German Period

Shortly after the German Imperial Government assumed control of Tanganyika (German East Africa) on 1 January 1891, the colonial administration upset this tenuous balance by adopting a wildlife preservation policy that restricted traditional African hunting practices. Governor Julius von Soden, a career diplomat known to Africans as Mr. Paper, because of his proclivity for paperwork, issued the first game regulations in 1891 for northern Tanganyika's Moshi District. This ordinance required African hunters to pay 500 rupees for permission to kill elephants.[10]

Five years later, Governor Hermann von Wissman, a big game hunter and early conservationist, enacted a more comprehensive game ordinance, which created two wild-life sanctuaries, one on Mount Kilimanjaro's western slopes, and one between the Rufiji River and the Rubehobeho country in east-central Tanganyika. This regulation also introduced a licensing system whereby African hunters could buy a basic shooting permit for five rupees, or an elephant and rhinoceros license for 500 rupees. It was unnecessary for Africans to have a license "to shoot animals trespassing on cultivated ground." A 1908 Hunting Ordinance established more game reserves; and, by the time of the 1919 British takeover, Tanganyika had twenty wildlife sanctuaries. Further regulations prohibited all shooting in these areas "without the special permission of the Imperial Government."[11]

As in Kenya and Uganda, the creation of game reserves and the imposition of a costly licensing system not only curbed the destruction of wild animals but also caused a fauna population crisis throughout the country. With an increased number of disease-carrying wild animals and the centuries-old equilibrium between man and tsetse fly altered by German game laws, sleeping sickness and nagana became more widespread. By 1906, sleeping sickness was well established along the shores of Lake Victoria and was spreading to the country around both ends of Lake Tanganyika. Two years later, Alexander Wollaston, a traveler and naturalist, reported that whole villages in the Lake Tanganyika region "have been wiped out [by the disease] and huge tracts of fertile land. . .which were

---

10. C.F.M. Swynnerton, "An Examination of the Tsetse Problem in North Mossurisse, Portuguese East Africa," *Bulletin of Entomological Research*, Vol. II (1921), p. 333.

11. Gosselin to Salisbury, 22 June 1896, FOCP 6849/229.

formally cultivated, have become impenetrable jungle." In 1911, another outbreak of sleeping sickness occurred along the Ruvuma River near Songea in southern Tanganyika.[12]

Dr. Feldman of the German medical corps believed that infected wild animals and tsetse flies entering the country from the Congo, Mozambique, and Rhodesia precipitated these incidents. Dr. Robert Koch, a government bacteriologist and entomologist, strengthened the theory that wild animals were entirely responsible for the presence of tsetse flies after he discovered that crocodiles were a favorite breeding ground of *G. Papalis*. As a result of Koch's findings, the colonial administration, under pressure from frustrated European farmers and officials, attempted to eradicate the country's crocodiles by offering a reward to anyone for crocodile eggs.[13]

Later, British entomologists abolished this program, claiming instead that sleeping sickness and nagana arose as "a consequence of quantitative changes in the relationships of three of the five populations involved—man, his domestic livestock, and the wild fauna—and the effects of these changes upon the remaining two populations, the trypanosomes and the tsetses."[14] The German colonial government had triggered these changes by enacting a game preservation law which caused an ecological catastrophe of frightening proportions:

> From the turn of the century many woodland savannah peoples suffered plagues of bush pigs and baboons which ruined their crops. Shortly afterwards lions and other predators multiplied, forcing the people to retreat from the forest fringes. The deserted fields relapsed to bush, soon intensified by tsetse flies. Cattle began to die of trypanosomiasis and men of a disease which developed from fever and lassitude to coma and death. Men and livestock retreated further. Pigs, lions, bush, and tsetses followed them. Nature was reconquering the land.[15]

The British Period

By the time the Great Powers had assigned Tanganyika to Great Britain as a mandated territory in 1919, the ecological situation had deteriorated even further. Thousands of acres of unattended European and African farmland had fallen into decay when the owners joined the military during World War I. Wild animals repopulated much of the

---

12. *Ibid.*; "Extract From Report on Tanganyika Territory," *Journal of the Societ for the Preservation of the Fauna of the Empire*, New Series Part II (July, 1922), p. 50.

13. D.F. Clyde, *History of the Medical Service of Tanganyika* (Dar es Salaam: Government Press, 1962), pp. 28-31; A.F.R. Wollaston, *From Ruwenzori to the Congo* (London: John Murray, 1908), p. 225.

14. Kjekshus, *Ecology Control*, pp. 167-8.

15. J. Ford, *The Role of Trypanosomiases in African Ecology* (Oxford: Clarendon Press, 1971), p. 494.

land, thereby extending the tsetse fly's range. With Tanganyika's economic, political, and transportation system all but destroyed as a result of the war, famine and influenza epidemics became widespread and added to the environmental problems.

Apart from the wider and more important issue of Tanganyika's reconstruction, the most perplexing problems confronting the British colonial administration between the two world wars were the preservation of the country's wildlife and the tsetse fly's eradication. As early as 1918, Sir Horace Byatt, Tanganyika's Administrator and first governor, noted Germany's long-standing commitment to wildlife preservation and intimated that he would pursue a similar policy:

> There is no doubt that German East Africa is as a whole...very rich in big game. The former German administration. . .made and zealously enforced laws for their protection and preservation. This is a principle with which I am entirely in sympathy, for although myself fond of shooting, a good many years' experience in various parts of Africa have convinced me that it is the duty of responsible authorities at the present day to prevent too great a reduction in the numbers of such animals.[16]

However, Byatt experienced difficulty in continuing the German policy.

One of the earliest displays of public hostility toward wild animals occurred when *The Pioneer: The British East Africa and Uganda News*, an influential Nairobi-based newspaper, railed against those who supported game preservation, claiming that there should be "a little more sympathy for the genus homo and less for the game."[17] Approximately two years later, the *Times* (London) warned, "Our great impediment to the protection of big game in many parts of Africa is the suspicion under which it lies of harbouring the tsetse fly."[18] By 1913, Major James Stevenson-Hamilton, a South African Game Warden, postulated the theory that wild animals were responsible for the presence of tsetse flies had become "so firmly fixed in the mind of the average man. . .that no amount of contrary argument or even proof could ever have much effect in altering his opinion."[19]

The work of many concerned individuals only confirmed this assessment. For example, when Sir W.H. Manning, a staunch conservationist, opposed wildlife destruction as a solution to the tsetse menace, he failed to gain popular support. The continuing conflict between anti-and pro-game groups forced the colonial administration to pursue an incongruous policy of eradicating the tsetse fly and preserving wild animals.

---

16. J. Iliffe, *A Modern History of Tanganyika* (Cambridge: Cambridge University Press, 1979), p. 163.

17. Byatt to Long, 2 October 1918, CO 691/16.

18. *The Pioneer. The British East Africa and Uganda News*, 5 September 1908, p. 1.

19. *The Times*, 13 June 1910, p. 11.

Charles Francis Massy Swynnerton, one of the most remarkable men to serve in Tanganyika, tried to strike a balance between these two extremes. Born on 3 December 1877, of missionary parents, young Swynnerton developed an interest in natural history at Lancing College in West Sussex and hoped to continue studying at Oxford. His parents, however, wanted him to go to South Africa to earn a proper living; so, in 1897, at the age of nineteen he arrived in Natal, alone, determined, and afraid. Shortly thereafter, he accepted employment as an assistant in a general store. Swynnerton soon resigned and, for the next twenty-one years, worked at different jobs, including farm manager, big game hunter, and amateur naturalist.

In June 1918, after a severe physical breakdown, Swynnerton signed a three-month contract with the Mozambique Company to survey tsetse distribution and habits in Mozambique's North Mossurise territory. His findings, published in the *Bulletin of Entomological Research*, yielded three conclusions that would be of benefit during his Tanganyika years: that concentrated human settlements could clear the land of *G. Brevipalpis* and *G. Pallidipes*; that properly controlled grass fires could restrict the spread of tsetse flies; and that *G. Morsitans*, one of the more common tsetse species, "might survive the destruction of all large mammalian life."[20]

On Byatt's recommendation, the Colonial Office appointed Swynnerton Director of Game Preservation, Tanganyika Territory, on 30 November 1919.[21] As a conservationist, Swynnerton was more practical than most and realized that stopping the tsetse fly could entail the extermination of certain wildlife species. Nevertheless, he worked tirelessly to preserve Tanganyika's fauna and searched continually for methods other than game destruction for eradicating the tsetse fly.[22]

Swynnerton's first significant accomplishment was to draft the Game Preservation Ordinance of 1921, which embodied most of the principles used in other British colonies. Apart from governing the sanctuaries established by the German colonial government, these regulations created Complete Reserves in which "no person shall hunt any animal"; and Partial Reserves in which "no person shall hunt game of the species declared. . .to be protected in those reserves." This ordinance also continued the German practice of limiting African hunters by outlawing the use of nets, guns, traps, snares, pit-falls, poison, or poison weapons. These restrictions, as with the German game laws, caused a fauna

---

20. J. Stevenson-Hamilton, "The Relation Between Game and Tsetse Flies," *Journal of the Society for the Preservation of the Wild Fauna of the Empire*, Vol. VI (1913), pp. 88-9.

21. The section on Swynnerton's life is based on an interview with H.F. Lamprey, 14 June 1979; and McKelvey, *Man against Tsetse*, pp. 134-56. Also, see Swynnerton, "Examination of the Tsetse Problem in North Mossurisse," pp. 376, 380-5.

22. Byatt to Milner, 10 July 1920, CO 691/33.2

population explosion and contributed to the spread of the tsetse fly. Six months after the enactment of the regulation, the colonial administration, hoping to correct this error, empowered Swynnerton to shoot or "authorise the killing of elephant, buffalo, hippopotamus or any animal which may become dangerous by reason of it being a carrier of tsetse fly, in such areas and in such numbers as the Governor may from time to time direct."[23]

Swynnerton's second major achievement was overseeing the growth of the Game Department. This was not an easy task. Many officials looked upon the Game Department as a "luxury" organization; whenever Tanganyika experienced budgetary problems it was usually the Game Department that suffered. During the 1937-1938 economic depression, for example, the colonial government considered abolishing the Department. Annual budget battles between the Game Warden and the Finance Committee in Dar es Salaam were invariably tense and—according to George Rushby, who joined the Game Department in 1938, and later became Deputy Game Warden—"extremely bitter."[24]

Nevertheless, through the sheer force of his personality, Swynnerton transformed the Game Department into East Africa's most effective wildlife preservation institution. When created in 1919, the Department's only purpose was the "preservation of animals in their natural state and in as large numbers as possible." By 1925, its mission had expanded to include: the protection of European and African cultivation against game; the study of the relationship between wildlife and the tsetse fly; and the reclamation of tsetse fly-infested land. The Department's European staff also grew under Swynnerton's leadership, from four Assistant Game Rangers in 1919 to eighteen positions in 1926, more than three times the number engaged by either Uganda or Kenya.[25]

Even more impressive was the fact that qualified scientists, including a microscopist, entomologist, and botanist staffed some of these positions. In 1928, Swynnerton added a trained zoologist to the Department. Moreover, he encouraged all of them to make specialized studies of particular wildlife species. Constantine Ionides, who joined the Department in 1933 as an elephant control officer, became a world renowned herpetologist. George Rushby specialized in elephants and published a number of articles in *Tanganyika Notes and Records*, including "The African Elephant and Its Hunters."[26] Swynnerton himself was a noted authority on rodents and lesser mammals.

---

23. Interview with Lamprey, 14 June 1979.

24. A copy of the ordinance is contained in Tanganyika Territory, *The Tanganyika Territory Gazette*, 16 December 1921; C.F.M. Swynnerton, "Memorandum on Game and Tsetse," enclosure in Hollis to Churchill, 17 May 1922, CO 691/55; Kjekshus, *Ecology Control*, p. 79.

25. G.G. Rushby, *No More the Tusker* (London: W.H. Allen, 1965), pp. 176-7; K. Caldwell, *Report on a Fauna Survey in Eastern and Central Africa* (London: Society for the Preservation of the Fauna of the Empire, Occasional Paper 8, 1948), p. 9.

26. This opinion was advanced in the interview with Lamprey, 14 June 1979. Also, see J.F.R. Hill, *Tanganyika: A Review of Its Resources and Their Development* (Dar es Salaam: Government Printer, 1955), p. 666-70.

Yet these achievements failed to result in greater wildlife protection. Prior to the Second World War, each Game Ranger patrolled an area about the size of Scotland. It was impossible for one ranger and his African scouts to safeguard wild animals in more than a quarter of such a large territory. Most Game Rangers, therefore, concentrated their efforts on preserving wildlife within the country's game reserves. Outside the sanctuaries, the District Commissioner—who served as veterinarian, postmaster, judge, police investigator, jailer, and often marriage counselor—was responsible for administering game laws and prosecuting violators. Given the heavy work load, most District Commissioners were indifferent toward wildlife and the Game Department.[27]

At times, this lack of interest caused catastrophes. In the late 1920s, the Mkalama government office in north-central Tanganyika organized a game drive in Iambi, which was nothing more than a wildlife killing expedition to eradicate the tsetse fly. The District Commissioner invited all interested Europeans hunters to come to Iambi on a certain Sunday to shoot any animal they desired. Truckloads of sportsmen passed the government station en route to the hunting ground. V.E. Johnson, a Lutheran missionary, beseeched the District Commissioner to change the day because he feared that trigger-happy hunters would needlessly destroy ordinary plains game such as antelopes, gazelles, giraffes, and zebras rather than known disease carriers like buffalo. The District Commissioner, however, refused to adjust the date and the slaughter took place. Thousands of non-disease carrier wild animals were killed.[28]

Swynnerton's investigation into the nature of the tsetse fly-wild animal relationship was to be his greatest feat. His research contributed significantly to wildlife preservation by demonstrating that game destruction would not necessarily result in eradication of the tsetse fly. Swynnerton began his work in 1921 when the government ordered him to conduct a tsetse fly distribution survey. Afterwards, he sketched a tsetse fly distribution map and started preliminary experiments at Kilosa in east central Tanganyika to determine the effect of previous grass burning on *G. Morsitans*.

Within a few months, a more serious situation confronted Swynnerton. In February 1922, Salim, the headman of Basheshi, reported to the authorities that sleeping sickness had broken out in Maswa District southeast of Lake Victoria. Dr. George Maclean, Medical Officer at Mwanza, investigated and discovered that the disease, which the local inhabitants

---

27. W.H. Mercer (ed.), *Colonial Office List 1926* (London: Waterlow & Sons Ltd., 1926), p. 451; W.H. Mercer (ed.), *Colonial Office List 1927* (London: Waterlow & Sons, 1927), p. 458; G.G. Rushby, "The African Elephant and Its Hunter," *Tanganyika Notes and Records*, No. 17 (June, 1944), pp. 59-63.

28. American Committee for International Wild Life Protection, *African Game Protection* (Cambridge, Mass., American Committee for International Wild Life Protection, 1933), p. 21; Rushby, *No More the Tusker*, p. 112; C.J.P. Ionides, *Mambas and Man-Eaters, A Hunter's Story* (New York: Holt, Rinehart and Winston, 1965), p. 61.

initially regarded as *safula* or hookworm, was sleeping sickness. Maclean then ordered the construction of hospitals in the district's fly-free zones.

Upon hearing of the epidemic, Swynnerton went to Maswa "to gain first-hand knowledge of the probable relationship of the game to such an outbreak."[29] He noted that several fauna areas crisscrossed the entire tsetse fly zone. The first wildlife concentration was north of the Duma River, through Ngasamo and Masa, and then southwards to the Maswa-Luguru area. To the north and east, most species, except elephant and situtunga, were present. South and west, in the woodlands closely associated with the epidemic, wild animals were comparatively scare.

To Swynnerton, this variation in fauna distribution suggested that wildlife was not necessarily solely responsible for spreading trypanosomiasis. He did not publicize this theory because he was unable to ascertain whether *T. Gambiense* or *T. Rhodesiense* brought about the epidemic. If the former West African strain was responsible, infected humans from the Congo or elsewhere could have brought the trypanosomes into Tanganyika; or, it could have been dormant in the Maswa area since the First World War when German authorities discovered sleeping sickness "among a small number of Belgian askaris who were prisoners of war." If the disease was the latter (Rhodesian variety), the infectious agent could have been carried into Tanganyika by soldiers or by a strain that arose from *T. Brucei*, which was common to wildlife. It also could have been present all along as a trypanosome pathogenic to man.[30]

Despite his refusal to express a public opinion regarding the origin of the deadly trypanosomes, Swynnerton seriously doubted that wild animals were solely responsible for the spread of sleeping sickness and nagana. As evidence, he cited the findings of several research scientists who had investigated earlier epidemics. During 1913-1914, the German physician, Dr. Max Taute, had informed the British government's Interdepartmental Committee on Sleeping Sickness that German East Africa's infectious districts were generally ones that were not very rich in game. Taute also had warned the committee that *G. Morsitans* could feed on humans as well as wild animals, and it was likely that the tsetse fly would use man as its chief blood supplier if all wildlife were killed. Dr. Alymer Mays—who had conducted a sleeping sickness survey for the British South Africa Company in Northern Rhodesia—advised the committee that most epidemics occurred "in the vicinity of man traffic routes" away from the game areas. In addition, Mays believed his findings supported the

---

29. V.E. Johnson, *Pioneering for Christ in East Africa* (Rock Island, Illinois: Augustana Book Concern, 1948), pp. 87-8.

30. C.F.M. Swynnerton, "Entomological Aspects of an Outbreak of Sleeping Sickness Near Mwanza, Tanganyika Territory," *Bulletin of Entomological Research*, Vol. 13 (1923), p. 318.

view that the disease was transmitted "from man to man rather than that game [was] the chief reservoir."[31]

On the basis of this testimony and his own findings, Swynnerton rejected the fly-wildlife-man connection, claiming instead that:

> The trypanosome does not gain and may not keep up its full infectivity for man in places in which the fly does not depend, or ceases to depend, on man for its food; further, that man, at least for all practical purposes, is the only reservoir; and that it comes into definite contact with a fauna population that is sufficient to break freely the continuity of the attendance of the fly on man, and reduce its avidity. . .The presence of game would thus be protective to man.[32]

Swynnerton realized this theory would be unpopular among Africans and Europeans who lived in affected areas and believed that wildlife eradication was the only way to eliminate the tsetse fly. He therefore included in his Maswa report an eloquent refutation of the anti-game position, remarking that the extermination of wild animals over extensive areas by specially employed game control officers was simply "too expensive to contemplate," and that, unless the region in question was fully settled by humans, it gradually would fill with fauna again. Swynnerton also maintained that to arm Africans and allow unlimited shooting as in pre-colonial days undoubtedly would succeed in eradicating the larger un-gulates and carnivores but would leave bush-pigs and other small animals free to roam the country and spread the disease. Instead, he recommended the establishment of a broad human settlement strip between game and fly because he felt the latter inevitably used a tree or bush as a resting place between feedings on fauna and cattle.[33]

The Maswa epidemic provided Swynnerton with an opportunity to launch a full-scale investigation of the tsetse menace. On 17 May 1922, he submitted a memorandum to the Colonial Office, reviewing the events of the past year and outlining his future research plans. As part of his strategy, he exhorted the British government to take cognizance of the fact that Tanganyika offered exceptional advantages "as the final home of the Empire's African Game [because] vast areas of it will never be claimed for European settlement." To refute those who accused him of favoring game preservation at any cost, Swynnerton pointed out that he had recommended killing buffalo near Namanyere and expected to propose similar measures elsewhere in the territory. He again warned that wildlife was not the only disease carrier and indicated that cars, trains, and bicycles transported the tsetse fly all over

---

31. *Ibid.*, p. 324.

32. Quoted in *Ibid.*, p. 349.

33. *Ibid.*, pp. 350-1.

Tanganyika. Lastly, Swynnerton expressed the belief that, because of the tsetse population's size and variety, Tanganyika was ideal "for scientific and thorough experimentation which will give us the real solution of the tsetse problem."[34]

As soon as he returned to Tanganyika from leave in 1923, Swynnerton selected Tabora's Shinyanga subdistrict as the first experimental area and proceeded to put his views on game and the tsetse fly to a practical test. Shinyanga, a gently undulating country with rich soil, produced cotton, foodcrops, and groundnuts while its grasslands supported about 345,000 cattle. At the time of Swynnerton's investigation, approximately half the district was depopulated because of the fly's presence, and this portion, according to local inhabitants, contained the best soil and pasture. Numerous wildlife species, including impala, eland, giraffe, steinbuck, dikdik, zebra, wildebeest, hartebeest, and wart-hog, abounded while at least four different tsetse flies—*G. Palpalis*, *G. Pallidipes*, *G. Morsitans*, and *G. Swynnertoni*—roamed over the area, competing for food and space. After some preliminary investigations, Swynnerton discovered that the fly was steadily extending its range at the expense of Shinyanga's 150,000 human inhabitants:

> Everywhere on the edges of the cattle-areas there was the same advance of the young bush and the tsetse, and everywhere inside them are still the live roots of the suppressed bush. The natives themselves were highly alarmed, and some said. . .'Where will the end be?' I replied, 'Unless you stand firm and yourselves attack, the end will be in little more than twenty years.'[35]

Swynnerton eventually chose an abandoned German fort, built in 1912, for his Shinyanga headquarters. Although it was poorly located for research on *G. Morsitans*, the most common tsetse fly, it was ideally situated for the study of *G. Swynnertoni*, which dominated Shinyanga. After surveying the region, he concluded that sleeping sickness was transmitted most readily from man to fly to man through traffic and trade between Shinyanga's scattered villages. As for nagana, Swynnerton noted that local herdsmen incurred the greatest losses when they pushed cattle into fly zones late each dry season in search of food and water.[36]

Using these findings, Swynnerton formulated an anti-tsetse fly strategy which excluded mass destruction of wildlife. In November 1923, he presented the plan's first phase to a group of Africans in a meeting at Kizumbi. He told them that the situation could be improved by using pangas to clear the young bush in the margins of the settled areas each year. Six months later, a massive bush-clearing campaign got under way. With

---

34. *Ibid.*, pp. 357-8.

35. Swynnerton, "Memorandum on Game and Tsetse."

36. C.F.M. Swynnerton, "An Experiment in Control of Tsetse-Flies at Shinyanga, Tanganyika Territory," *Bulletin of Entomological Research*, Vol. 15 (1925), pp. 318-9.

the assistance of a research team assembled by Swynnerton, which included B.D. Burtt, a botanist; John F.V. Phillips, an ecologist; W.H. Potts, C.H.N. Jackson, and T.A.M. Nash, entomologists; G. St. Clair Thompson, a forester; and S.P. Teare, Game Ranger. Local people also participated on an unprecedented scale, thanks largely to the efforts of their leaders. Chiefs Ikomba, Makwaia, Makolo, and Luhende furnished 4,500 men; four western chiefdoms supplied 2,000; and Chiefs Mahizi and Masanja sent 1,400.[37]

As the campaign progressed, some workers tired and left, but in all, more than 10,000 worked on the project during the first season.[38] Considering the experimental nature of Swynnerton's work, they accomplished a great deal. In Kizumbi, men cleared a place "for many cattle" and provided a site for a new ploughing school. They also created a seven-mile-long fly-free corridor connecting the western and eastern chiefdoms, and reclaimed "many square miles of grazing land."[39]

The second phase of Swynnerton's plan sought to prevent people and game from carrying tsetse flies into the recently cleared Kizumbi cattle country. He achieved this by restricting travel to grazing grounds to persons from open country villages. Guards stationed on the main road checked all wayfarers and motorized vehicles entering Kizumbi. Colonial authorities closed several minor paths to the grazing grounds and prohibited direct passage between the bush and the ploughing school's pasture. After consultation with African cattle owners, the administration encouraged everyone traveling to or from Kizumbi to make periodic checks of their clothing for tsetse flies. Specially appointed game control officers killed all wildlife caught entering the experimental zone.[40]

These measures failed to satisfy dissidents, such as Dr. John B. Davey, who favored mass wildlife destruction as the only way to eradicate the tsetse fly. Davey, a government physician, characterized Swynnerton "as one interested in game preservation who has, with masterly hand, marshaled a formidable array of facts and theory to exculpate the game. . .moreover he believes. . .the much-needed experiment in game destruction has, for practical purposes, been carried out, and that we know the result."[41] In Tanganyika's *1924 Annual Medical Report*, Davey also noted the proximity of the epidemic foci to heavy wildlife concentrations and suggested a possible connection.[42] Swynnerton anticipated this criticism in his final Shinyanga report:

---

37. *Ibid.*, p. 319.

38. *Ibid.*, pp. 213-2.

39. *Ibid.*, p. 322.

40. *Ibid.*, pp. 322-3.

41. *Ibid.*, p. 326.

42. J.B. Davey, "The Outbreak of Human Trypanosomiasis (Trypanosoma Rhodesiense Infection) in Mwanza District, Tanganyika Territory," *Transactions of the Royal Society of Tropical Medicine and Hygiene*, Vol. 17 (1924), p. 475.

The relations of the fly and the game are not being ignored. They are being studied and will be the subject of special experimentation and, if necessary, of special localised measures fitted into our general scheme of control.[43]

The East African Committee, appointed by the British government to advise upon the potential for economic development of all central and east Africa territories, resolved this conflict in Swynnerton's favor after a delegation visited Shinyanga and registered satisfaction with his work. Shortly thereafter, the British government established in London the Tsetse Fly Committee of the Economic Advisory Council. This committee had two investigatory bodies, one in Nigeria administered by Dr. W.B. Johnson and Dr. L.L. Lloyd, and the other in Tanganyika under Swynnerton. Immediately after the committee's creation, Swynnerton started assembling a scientific team of entomologists, botanists, zoologists, and field officers to serve in Tanganyika's Game Department. By 1929, work had become so specialized that the colonial administration had converted the Game Department's Tsetse Division into a separate organization, with its headquarters at Kondoa-Irangi in central Tanganyika.[44] Swynnerton was responsible for this Division while I.U. Battye replaced him as Game Warden.

Swynnerton hoped these changes would give him time to resolve the tsetse fly issue, thus striking a blow for game preservation. Success, however, depended on uncontrollable human demographic trends. Thousands of acres of tsetse-infested bush could be cleared, but, if the land remained unpopulated and underdeveloped, it would soon revert to bushland. He also realized that regions with population densities as low as one person per square mile could not mount an adequate anti-tsetse campaign. Twenty-five persons per square mile, on the other hand, was sufficient to clear land of bush and till the soil, thereby reducing but not eliminating the tsetse fly's operational range. One hundred people per square mile produced a fly-free zone large enough to protect inhabitants from spreading sleeping sickness amongst themselves. Given Tanganyika's average population density of less than fifteen per square mile, it was inevitable that *T. Rhodesiense* flourished. Indeed, by 1931, it already had caused major epidemics near Lake Rukwa in Iringa Province and in nearly all of Kigoma and Tabora Provinces south of Mwanza.[45]

The continued spread of the tsetse fly failed to discourage Swynnerton. He plunged ahead with his work at Shinyanga, and eventually devised three options to stop the tsetse

---

43. Tanganyika Territory, *Medical Department Annual Report* (Dar es Salaam: Government Press, 1925), p. 44.

44. Swynnerton, "Shinyanga," p. 337.

45. C.F.M. Swynnerton, *The Tsetse Flies of East Africa* (London: Royal Entomological Society, 1936), p. 10.

fly. The first was a retreat from fly zones into concentrated human settlements which would keep the bush and tsetse fly under reasonable control. The wildlife destruction strategy proposed the complete eradication to eliminate the tsetse fly. The balanced approach advocated the tsetse fly's expulsion from large bushland areas without totally destroying the woodland, and the establishment of wider African settlements. Although this course of action recognized the need for "discriminative game expulsion," it rejected the total extermination concept.

Swynnerton dismissed the first option because it eventually required the despoliation of Tanganyika's forests. As far as wildlife destruction was concerned, he once again pointed out that, while such a tactic might work in certain limited open types of wooding, it could not be applied everywhere because of the high cost of hiring professional hunters. To allow unrestricted killing by Africans, according to Swynnerton, would have encouraged the spread of the tsetse fly by the movements of man and game which this kind of hunting engendered. He therefore supported the balanced approach as the "only full solution" available to the colonial administration. In large infected regions (e.g. 500 miles by 300 miles), Swynnerton proposed that the land be surveyed to determine vegetational, agricultural, and tsetse fly patterns, and then subdivided into smaller, more manageable parts before attacking the tsetse fly. Where sufficient people were available, he favored "the judiciously sited concentration of scattered villages" to achieve a population density of at least one hundred people per square mile.

The authorities then would help these villages gradually extend their borders until they coalesced with other settlements or natural barriers to form an effective defense system. Swynnerton also intended these "concentrated" villages to facilitate the growth and development of public services such as schools and hospitals. Moreover, he planned to introduce new agricultural and husbandry methods to improve the general economic well-being of the affected areas. After the colonial administration approved Swynnerton's strategy, Dr. George Maclean, a Sleeping Sickness Officer, started an anti-tsetse campaign based on a so-called "hexagon scheme," which was nothing more than a rotation system and six years of fallow at selected sites throughout Tanganyika. Maclean calculated that each family could keep eight to twelve acres free from the tsetse fly.[46]

Initially, the response to the "concentrated" village strategy was favorable. In 1933, the Provincial Commissioner of Kigoma Province reported that the Ha people's resettlement marked "a revolution in their tribal life" and simplified their transformation into "a disciplined and prosperous community."[47] J.P. Moffat, the officer who supervised the 1936-

---

46. McKelvey, *Man against Tsetse*, pp. 150-1.

47. G. MacLean, "Sleeping Sickness Measures in Tanganyika Territory," *Kenya and East Africa Medical Journal*, (1930), p. 123.

1937 concentration of 1,000 families in Urambo east of Tabora, claimed the people involved in the move were "happy and content" and "genuinely pleased with their new surroundings."[48] F.I.C. Apted, another Sleeping Sickness Officer, disclosed that the settlements caused a decline in the number of new infections from more than 3,000 to fewer than 600 by 1936.[49]

Swynnerton did not live to see the full economic and social impact of his scientific findings. On 8 June 1938, during a routine aerial game survey, Swynnerton and his botanist, Burtt, crashed in the bush near Singida.[50] His death marked the end of an era, both in terms of game preservation and tsetse fly research. Initially, the application of Swynnerton's scientific knowledge slowed wildlife destruction and convinced many government officials that killing wild animals would not stop the spread of sleeping sickness or nagana. But with Swynnerton out of the picture, anti-game sentiment among farmers gradually intensified.

Seven years after his death, two of Swynnerton's former colleagues, Potts and Jackson, undertook another experiment at Shinyanga to determine once and for all whether shooting hoofed game animals would eliminate the tsetse fly. To prevent the movement of fauna in and out of the six hundred-square-mile test site, Potts and Jackson selected a region bounded on three sides by village settlements. As the fourth side bordered on a grassy plain grazed by cattle and game, they hoped to keep wildlife out by shooting; but eventually found it necessary to build a fifty mile-long barbed wire fence to accomplish the task. To remove the wild animals from this area, professional hunters killed more than 8,500 beasts, including zebras, rhinoceroses, giraffes, buffaloes, and several antelope species.[51]

In terms of tsetse fly eradication, the Shinyanga research was a success. *G. Morsitans* and *G. Swynnertoni* disappeared completely while *G. Pallidipes* "was either exterminated or very heavily reduced." The cost of implementing the program was £50 per square mile, much less than the price of a bush clearing campaign. Potts and Jackson pointed out, however, that expenses would have been "enormously greater were it not for the fact that the tsetse site was isolated by villages and a fence for the greater part of the experiment."

48. Tanganyika Territory, *Provincial Commissioners Annual Report 1933* (Dar es Salaam: Government Printer, 1934), pp. 77-8.

49. J.P. Moffet, "A Strategic Retreat From the Tse Tse Fly; Uyowa and Bugoma Concentrations 1937," *Tanganyika Notes and Records*, No. 7 (1939), p. 37.

50. F.I.C. Apted, "Sleeping Sickness in Tanganyika, Past, Present, and Future," *Transactions of the Royal Society of Tropical Medicine and Hygiene*, Vol. LVI, (1962), p. 16.

51. For Swynnerton's obituary, see *Tanganyika Notes and Records*, No. 6 (December, 1938), pp. 3-4; *Journal of the Society for the Preservation of the Fauna of the Empire*, New Series Part XXXIV, (August, 1938), pp. 17-8. For a report on the Shinyanga experiment, see W.H. Potts and C.H.N. Jackson, "The Shinyanga Game Destruction Experiment," *Bulletin of Entomological Research*, Vol. XLIII, (July, 1952), pp. 365-374.

Moreover, they concluded that professional hunters would have to continue shooting indefinitely or the colonial administration would have to erect and maintain a game-proof fence, or else the wildlife and then the tsetse fly would return to Shinyanga. On the basis of these findings—which vindicated Swynnerton's earlier work—Potts and Jackson told the authorities that "game destruction is not recommended except in isolated areas of manageable size."[52]

Despite the Tsetse Research Department's continued work, however, control of sleeping sickness and nagana remained an elusive goal. As late as 1949, Dr. John F.V. Phillips informed Governor Sir Edward Twining that "there is more fly today than there was twenty years ago in Tanganyika!"[53] On a more positive note, Potts and Jackson finally convinced the colonial administration that wholesale wildlife destruction would not eliminate the tsetse fly. Ironically, as the threat to wild animals lessened, crop raiding intensified.

In the southern portion of Rufiji District, for example, an agricultural report indicated that eland herds regularly grazed in African maize, millet, and cotton fields, causing severe damage.[54] People living in Rufiji's Matumbi and Muhoro areas complained to W.J. Macmillan, the District Officer, that "Native Cultivation guards pay no attention to complaints of damage being done by game." Apart from ordering more guards to protect crops "while their ammunition lasts," Macmillan promised little in the way of relief.[55]

Similar situations existed all over the country. In many regions crop protection was a greater problem than the tsetse fly. Therefore Tanganyika, like Kenya and Uganda, was faced with the difficult dilemma of how to control the tsetse fly and encourage economic development without eradicating wildlife. Devising a realistic solution required nearly all the colonial administration's efforts and energies.

---

52. Potts and Jackson, "Shinyanga Game Destruction Experiment," p. 365.

53. Ibid., pp. 373-4.

54. Rufiji District Book/Morongoro (Eastern Province) Vol. IV, Tanzania National Archives: No. 7-8.

55. Ibid.

CHAPTER IV

National Parks: The Dream

As previously mentioned, wildlife enthusiasts in East Africa and throughout the world believed that national parks would create a stable and harmonious man-animal balance without disturbing the region's social and economic development. In February 1939, Captain Keith Caldwell advanced this idea by telling the Conference of Game Wardens in Nairobi that national parks would "give greater promise of permanence and freedom from disturbance" than any other method of game preservation.[1]

Despite this optimism, the destruction and poaching of wild animals continued unabated. In May 1960, Elspeth Huxley, an observer of East African affairs for more than forty years, indicated that in Tanganyika "game has been virtually wiped out of large areas" and in Kenya the situation was "little better."[2] Later that year, the Board of Trustees of Tanganyika's national parks bemoaned the "considerable amount of pessimism voiced in the press and elsewhere as to the chances of saving the game of East Africa from rapid extinction."[3]

Several factors contributed to the national parks' inability to provide "permanence and freedom from disturbance" for East Africa's dwindling wildlife. Ever-increasing pressure from farmers and big game hunters took its toll of wild animals; but, the parks themselves created a more serious ecological imbalance by attracting thousands of tourists. In 1946, for example, the number of people visiting Kenya's game sanctuaries barely exceeded a few hundred, primarily because there was a lack of suitable hotels, restaurants, and swimming pools. By the end of 1955, more than 120,000 tourists had flocked to the country's national parks, which, by then, furnished a wide range of amenities for tourists.[4] Since most national parks were hours from a town or village, the trustees provided housing for the thousands of employees needed to ensure smooth functioning of these conveniences.

---

1. Report of Proceedings of a Conference of Game Wardens (held at Nairobi, 9-10 February, 1939), CO 323/1688.

2. E. Huxley, "Notes on Wildlife in East Africa," unpublished manuscript in author's possession, pp. 1, 3.

3. Tanganyika National Parks, *Reports and Accounts of the Board of Trustees 1960* (Arusha: Beauchamp Printing Co., Ltd., 1961), p. 7.

4. Colony and Protectorate of Kenya, *Legislative Council Debates*, Vol LXIX, Fifth Session, 23 May 1956 (Nairobi: Government Printer, 1956), p. 585.

The chimpanzee inhabits rain, swamp and montane forests; and dry forests and savannas with scattered trees.

Courtesy of Gerald Rilling

The demand for ivory brought the elephant to the verge of extinction. However, after a moratorium on international trade in ivory, agreed under the Convention on International Trade in Endangered Species (CITES) came into effect in January 1999, elephant populations have increased throughout many areas in East Africa.

Courtesy of Gerald Rilling

A Young lion at the Nairobi animal orphange.

Coutresy of the author

The stately giraffe, which reaches heights of eighteen to twenty feet, often posed a threat to telegraph wires in early colonial East Africa.

Courtesy of the author

The authorities also built unpaved tracks to allow tourists access to parts of the parks heretofore closed to humans. When the rains came—and during the dry season in places of volcanic ash soil—tracks became so rutted that drivers had to use ground on either side of them, thus widening the tracks and sometimes destroying vegetation which increased the possibility of irreparable soil erosion. Thus, in their eagerness to fulfill that part of the 1933 convention stating the "facilities shall, so far as possible, be given to the general public for observing the fauna and flora in national parks," the trustees unwittingly created a serious man-animal conflict within the latter's sanctuaries.[5]

In addition, national parks contributed to the negative attitude many Africans held toward wildlife in general and the parks in particular. Ever since the rise of British colonial rule, Africans had resented and resisted the imposition of game regulations. In 1959, for example, District Commissioner Charles Chenevix-Trench reported that, because the colonial administration had refused to pay compensation for wildlife damage, the Samburu people felt "more sore about the Government's game policy than about any other subject." Moreover, Chenevix-Trench believed it was hopeless to expect the "smallest cooperation" in any preservation project.[6] T.A. Watts, Commissioner for Machakos District, declared that the Kamba people of south central Kenya "consider all game animals as a menace to their crops and the livestock."[7]

These complaints were minor when compared to those of the Maasai people who occupied vast stretches of game country in southwestern Kenya and northwestern Tanganyika. The Maasai are primarily a pastoral people who regard their flocks, especially cattle, as a source of wealth and prestige. Their attitude toward wild animals that competed with domestic stock for grazing and water had been a subject of concern to the colonial administration since the turn of the century.

In 1907, John H. Patterson, Kenya's first Game Ranger, argued that, because Maasai cattle herds "eat up everything," the Laikipia Plateau north of the Uganda Railway was a wasteland as far as wildlife was concerned.[8] On 4 April 1911, the colonial authorities persuaded the Maasai to evacuate this region and move south of the railway to make way for European settlers. This new area—9,210 square miles, or more than twice the size of

---

5. E. Walter Russell, *A Management Policy for the Tanzania National Parks* (London: Fauna Preservation Society, 1968), pp. 19-20. Also, see Great Britain, *Agreements Concluded at the International Conference for the Protection of the Fauna and Flora of Africa*, Cmd. 4453 (London: HMSO, 1933), p. 24.

6. Samburu District Annual Report 1959, KNA: SAM/4.

7. Machakos District Annual Report 1959, KNA: DC/MKS/1/1/35.

8. J.H. Patterson, "A Report From British East Africa," *Journal of the Society for the Preservation of the Wild Fauna of the Empire* Vol. III (1907), p. 73.

the old Laikipia Reserve—was in the Loita/Mara region in southern Kenya. Even before the Maasai moved, John Ainsworth, then Provincial Commissioner of Nyanza, warned his superiors that wildlife had overrun parts of Maasailand, and were "a source of considerable inconvenience" to the people. He suggested adoption of a scheme whereby big game hunters would shoot the wild animals while the administration would export the hides and meat. Ainsworth also maintained that, despite the fact that Maasailand's eastern border coincided with the Southern Game Reserve "it was necessary to regard Masai [sic] interests as paramount" throughout the entire region.[9]

Over the next several decades, the Maasai continued to complain about wildlife. Hyena packs frequently raided villages, killing sheep and calves. Cattle were highly susceptible to malignant catarrah, *engeeya oingati*, which was spread on grass by the afterbirth on wildebeest calves. Other cattle diseases associated with wild animals included rinderpest, anthrax, black quarter, and brucellosis. Wildlife also competed for scarce water, and contributed to Maasailand's desiccation by their eating habits. The 1935 *Masai Annual Report*, noted:

> The game do not ruin the grazing themselves but force the cattle to do so, they nibble off the tops and pass on while the cattle come behind and complete the destruction. Any plan for rotational resting of grasslands during seeding time is doomed to failure while vast herds of game roam at will.[10]

The colonial administration tried to rectify some of these problems by adopting control measures. In 1938, Jack Bonham, a big game hunter who later became Game Ranger of Coast Province, killed some 8,000 zebra and 5,000 wildebeest at Narok to provide extra grazing land for cattle and reduce the incidence of malignant catarrah. The following year, hunters shot 1,500 wildebeests to stop the spread of this disease. In 1975, Ole Sindiyo, a Maasai Game Warden, summed up his people's attitude toward fauna:

> We have to share our land with wild and dangerous animals. We have to learn to give way to the elephant, the rhinoceros, the lion, etc., and this has not been our way of life. Many of us have lost children, others have lost stock and relatives to these wild animals which belong to the government. The government has value for these animals but they are of no value to us. . .The value of wildlife being gone, we know of no other value whatever and yet our cattle are either being killed or injured by these animals

---

9. The best account of this period remains G.R. Sandford, *An Administrative and Political History of the Masai Reserve* (London: Waterlow and Sons, Ltd., 1919).

10. Masai Annual Report 1935, KNA: PC/SP 1/2/2. Also, see Masai Annual Report 1921, KNA: PC/SP 1/2/2; Masai Annual Report 1924, KNA: PC/SP 1/2/2; and Masai Annual Report 1925, KNA: PC/SP 1/2/2.

for food. . .The presence of these animals in our districts means loss of lives and stock every year and nothing else.[11]

In Kenya, such feelings threatened to precipitate a crisis at Amboseli, a rich 1,259-square-mile game region at the foot of Mount Kilimanjaro. As it was part of the Maasai Land Unit and contained the only water available for many miles, the Maasai and their cattle used it for most of the year. By 1956, the competition for water between domestic livestock and fauna had caused considerable land damage:

> As a result of the constant pounding of the hooves of thousands of cattle, vegetation and soil structure are rapidly being destroyed and if allowed to continue this will inevitably result not only in the total elimination of wild animals but also in the area becoming practically useless from the point of view of the Maasai themselves.[12]

The Maasai opposed the creation of a national park at Amboseli for several reasons even though the colonial administration assured them that the park would resolve all their problems. A national park would have meant that the land around Amboseli Lake and swamps would be excised from the Maasai Land Unit—this the Maasai refused to do. A more significant objection concerned the fact that Amboseli furnished dry-weather grazing for livestock. In addition, the Maasai believed that Amboseli's swamp and spring water contained medicinal salts which their herds needed.[13]

Because of this resistance, the colonial administration placed Amboseli under the control of the Trustees of the Royal National Parks of Kenya in November 1948, as a park adjunct (later known as a national reserve). The trustees had "the care and responsibility of the fauna and flora, and the right to retain them, so far as may be possible, in their pristine condition." To protect the Maasai and their cattle, the trustees had to "do all in their power to prevent inconvenience to human rights as a result of the privileges they are granted."[14]

Such opposing responsibilities inevitably led to a conflict of interests, which, in turn, caused a further diminution of wild animals. In times of drought, as in 1955, there was fierce competition for grass and water. Colonial officials serving in the area believed the

---

11. P. Matthiessen and E. Porter, *The Tree Where Man Was Born: The African Experience* (New York: Cresent, 1975), p. 123. Also, see Masai Annual Report 1938, KNA: PC/SP 1/2/2 and Masai Annual Report 1939, KNA: PC/SP 1/2/2.

12. Kenya Wild Life Society, *First Annual Report 1956* (Nairobi: W. Boyd and Co., Ltd., 1957), pp. 46-7.

13. Kenneth Cowley, formerly Provincial Commissioner of Kenya's Southern Province, to author, 18 September 1979, private correspondence in author's possession.

14. Colony and Protectorate of Kenya, *Second Interim Report of the Game Policy Committee* (Nairobi: Government Printer, 1945), p. 17.

only way of preserving game was to convince the Maasai that "it was in their own interests to look after the wildlife and profit from it because of its great attraction for tourists." To help create a more positive Maasai attitude, the Game Policy Committee recommended the abolition of the Amboseli National Reserve and the establishment of a Game Reserve Committee. The latter, a policy making body, included representatives from the colonial administration, Game Department, national parks organization, and Maasai nation. By encouraging Maasai participation, officials hoped the Amboseli matter would improve gradually, with wild animals and cattle sharing the same limited resources.[15]

By the end of 1958, the Game Department reported the Maasai attitude toward wildlife had deteriorated to such an extent that most of them favored destruction of all wild animals in Amboseli. To lessen Maasai hostility, the colonial administration financed a project to provide permanent watering points for cattle which congregated in Amboseli. The daily coming and going of the cattle threatened to turn the areas to/from and around the water holes into a dust bowl. It also mounted a publicity campaign to persuade the Maasai that there was money in game. For their part, Maasai elders agreed to form a game committee to study Amboseli's ecological problems.[16] In addition, African District Council members promised to support game preservation "if they were given some say in their own district and some financial compensation." The colonial administration acceded to these requests and, on 14 July 1961, Sir Patrick Renison, Kenya's Governor turned over the Maasai Amboseli Game Reserve to the Kajiado African District Council, telling the Maasai:

> Each animal. . .is worth many thousands of shillings to you and your Council if it remains alive; but dead it is worth only a few shillings to the selfish and miserable poachers who killed it. I hope therefore that you will take the sternest measures to prevent and stamp out this illegal theft of your assets.[17]

The Maasai Amboseli Game Reserve was an immediate attraction. Between 1 July and 1 November 1961, 5,668 people paid 58,885 shillings in admission fees.[18] Ironically, the following year, the Game Department indicated that Amboseli's popularity had opened another chapter in the tragic story of man's age-old struggle with East Africa's wild animals:

15. Cowley to author, 18 September 1979; Colony and Protectorate of Kenya, *Report of the 1956 Game Policy Committee, Sessional Paper No. 7* (Nairobi: Government Printer, 1958), pp. 24-5.

16. Kajiado District *Annual Report 1959*, KNA: PC/SP/1/5/6.

17. "Masai Tribe Takes Over Amboseli Game Reserve," *Wild Life* (September/December, 1961), p. 50. A copy of Renison's speech is contained in Renison Papers, Rhodes House, Oxford, MSS. BRIT. EMP. 5404.

18. Colony and Protectorate of Kenya, *Game Department Annual Report 1961* (Nairobi: Government Printer, 1962), p. 4.

As a result of the present popularity of the reserve. . .many areas are now churning up seas of dust, resembling tank training courses, and the last vestiges of grazing and of cover are being removed. If this is not to result in the disappearance of the animals on which the fauna of Amboseli rests, immediate action must be taken, and that action can only be. . .the restriction of cars.[19]

The Maasai's presence in Serengeti caused even more of a disappointment. During the three years after the creation of the Serengeti National Park in 1951, low rainfall limited cattle grazing. To make matters worse, alternate water supplies provided by the colonial administration were unfit for consumption. The Maasai therefore concentrated their herds in the Crater Highlands and Moru Kopjes where there was adequate grass and water. As wild animals also sought nourishment in these oases, there were clashes between Maasai herders and park authorities.

When attempts to solve these problems failed, the Board of Trustees concluded that the continued presence of the Maasai and their livestock was a danger to the well-being of Serengeti's fauna. They also realized that Serengeti, embracing more than 4,800 square miles, was unmanageable and far too ambitious. The trustees proposed to reconstitute several places in Serengeti as "true" national parks free from human interests. These included the Ngorongoro region in the Northern Province, approximately 540 square miles; the ten-square mile Embagai Crater, also in the Northern Province; and the western Serengeti in the Lake Province, about 1,400 square miles.

The central Serengeti plains, which comprised more than 2,600 square miles, was to be excised from the national park and protected by special legislation. This plan, while providing free access for the Maasai and their herds, would have prohibited all development which "might lead to permanent settlement or interfere with the normal migration and seasonal grazing of game, or be in any way inimical to game." The Crater Highlands and the Moru Kopjes would be development areas where wildlife interests would be subordinated to those of man. The colonial administration also promised to furnish permanent water supplies and improved pasturage in these areas to replace those in the Ngorongoro and Embagai Craters which would no longer be available to the Maasai.[20]

One month after the trustees announced this program, the Tanganyika and Kenya Wild Life Societies published *Comments on the Tanganyika Government's White Paper Entitled "The Serengeti Park."* It criticized Tanganyika's colonial administration, the Board

19. Colony and Protectorate of Kenya, *Game Department Annual Report 1962* (Nairobi: Government Printer, 1963), p. 5.

20. Tanganyika Territory, *The Serengeti National Park* (Dar es Salaam: Government Printer, 1956), pp. 1-4.

of Trustees, and the Maasai for concluding a behind-the-scenes agreement, claiming that "the proposals set out in the *White Paper* [did] not constitute a satisfactory solution to the present problem from the point of view of game protection."

The Fauna Preservation Society also rejected the *White Paper*, and proposed that an independent survey be conducted before any changes were made in the Serengeti National Park. The Fauna Preservation Society suggested the matter be discussed at a conference of the International Union for the Conservation of Nature and Natural Resources, which was about to open in Edinburgh, Scotland.[21] Indeed, the Union's General Assembly subsequently adopted a resolution calling for an investigation of the Serengeti issue. The Fauna Preservation Society arranged for a review to be carried out in November and December 1956, under the leadership of Dr. W.H. Pearsall, Director of the East African Agriculture and Forestry Research Organization. His report claimed the proposed national parks were too small to be ecologically self-sufficient and inadequate for game preservation.[22]

Tanganyika's colonial administration therefore appointed a commission of inquiry on 3 April 1957, to consider conditions in the Serengeti National Park, examine the *White Paper* proposals, and recommend modifications. The committee's report supported Pearsall's findings, claiming that the Serengeti National Park "must cover an area large enough to provide a viable ecological unit embracing the full cycle of animal migration."[23] The report also caused consternation among the Maasai, who had accepted the *White Paper's* proposals because the authorities had promised to develop adequate alternate water supplies. According to the commission, porous soil made surface water storage impracticable and high fluorine content made subsurface supplies unfit for consumption.[24]

Upon learning of the report, Oltimbau Ole Masiaya, a Maasai spokesman, criticized the colonial administration:

> . . .the stage has been reached where we no longer feel masters in our own country but rather that we live there on sufferance only. Masai value personal freedom above anything else, but in the National Park we are not free.

He also pointed out that the government agreed to furnish new water supplies if the Maasai abandoned Ngorongoro and Embagai Craters, but this was not done. He warned

---

21. Tanganyika and Kenya Wild Life Societies, *Comments on the Tanganyika Government's White Paper Entitled "The Serengeti Park"* (Nairobi: D.A. Hawkins Ltd., 1956), p. 10.

22. W.H. Pearsall, *Report on an Ecological Survey of the Serengeti National Park* (London: Fauna Preservation Society, 1957), p. 75.

23. Tanganyika Territory, *Report of the Serengeti Committee of Enquiry, 1957* (Dar es Salaam: Government Printer, 1957), p. 1, 23.

24. *Ibid.*, p. 19.

the colonial administration that, if it was unable to find additional water, the 1955 agreement would be null and void. The Maasai then issued a statement insisting that people living in the Serengeti had certain rights, including freedom of movement, access to water and grazing lands, and the authority to defend lives and property against wild animals.[25]

To placate the Maasai, the colonial administration compromised. The new policy stated that recommendations to establish national parks or nature reserves in the Ngorongoro and Embagai Craters were unacceptable because it was improper "to seek Masai (sic) consent to a relinquishment of their rights in the two craters at the same time as they were giving up established rights within the Park itself." Instead, these places would become Conservation Units, administered by the government with the objective of conserving water, forest, and pasture. In exchange for a Maasai promise to evacuate the reconstituted Serengeti National Park, the colonial administration stipulated that "full compensation must be paid to all who are to be disturbed by the exclusion of human rights from the new park." Compensation took the form of a £35,000 fund which would be used to develop new water supplies in areas outside the park.[26] On 17 June 1958, the Legislative Council ended eighteen years of controversy by accepting these proposals and reconstituting the Serengeti National Park.

Although the resolution of the Serengeti problem signaled the completion of East Africa's national park system, it quickly became evident that these sanctuaries, like the old game reserves, were incapable of maintaining a harmonious man-animal balance. More importantly, establishment of national parks failed to prevent the illegal slaughter of wild animals. Throughout the post-World War II period, poaching remained the greatest cause of wildlife destruction in East Africa. The poachers, primarily Africans but some Europeans, used wild animals for a variety of products. They killed giraffes for their sinews to make bow strings and their tail hairs to fletch arrows; wildebeests for their tails, rhinoceroses for their horn, and elephants for their ivory. They shot other animals, including most species of gazelles and antelopes, for their meat.[27]

Poaching's most disturbing aspect was the appalling waste it created. Often, traps and snares were not inspected for weeks or months, leaving a trapped animal to rot in the sun. Fauna that fell into game pits died after a few days from lack of food and water. Another favorite poaching tactic was to prod entire herds into a continuous line of nooses

---

25. *Ibid.*, p. 3. Also, Oltimbau Ole Masiaya, Memorandum on the Serengeti National Park, p. 5, in Collection of Materials Pertaining to the Serengeti National Park, Rhodes House, Oxford, MSS. AFR. S 12376.

26. Tanganyika Territory, *Proposals for Reconstituting the Serengeti National Park* (Dar es Salaam: Government Printer, 1958), p. 2.

27. Kenya Wild Life Society, *Annual Report 1956*, p. 9.

George Dove, who was born in South Africa and moved to East Africa as a child, remained a big-game hunter throughout his life. Dove posed with this big tusker, which one of his clients shot while on safari in southern Tanzania in the 1950s.

Courtesy of Gerald Rilling

Tony Henley (as young man with Kenya Game Department). In 1948 he worked as a ranger for the Kenya Game Department. He shot this elephant while on safari.

Courtesy of Tony Henley

sometimes stretching for more than a mile. After a successful drive, poachers usually were unable to dispose of such huge quantities of meat, so many of the animals were hamstrung and left to be collected as needed. Normally, it was days before they were put out of their misery.[28]

In 1960, Lieutenant-Colonel Peter Molloy, Director of Tanganyika National Parks, estimated that, in addition to those animals killed by firearms, 150,000 beasts fell prey annually to snares in the Serengeti National Park. Indeed, approaches to water holes in dry seasons were so ringed by snares that few wild animals escaped alive; those that managed to get through to the water usually were killed by poachers lying in wait with poisoned arrows. In October 1960, an anti-poaching team sighted a gang of more than a hundred poachers, including women and children to carry meat, in Uganda's Murchison Falls National Park. Similar problems existed in Queen Elizabeth National Park, where rangers frequently surprised poaching gangs.[29] The situation in Kenya was so desperate that Sir Patrick Renison, the Governor, issued the following directive to all administrative officers:

---

28. *Ibid.*, pp. 9-10.

29. Huxley, Notes on Wildlife, p. 1. Also, see Uganda National Parks, *Report and Accounts of the Trustees of the Uganda National Parks 1961* (Kampala: Government Printer, 1962), p. 7.

I am disturbed by the grave threat to Kenya's wild life caused by the activities of poachers. These activities have recently become so extensive as to present a serious danger to the preservation of the game population of the Colony. Though it is primarily the responsibility of the Game Department to protect the Colony's game. . .I wish all officers and particularly those of the Administration and of the Police. . .to take all possible measures to put down poaching. I am sure that I can rely on all officers to apply themselves to this task. Kenya's game population, although unhappily diminished during the past two decades, is still a great natural asset and it is of the first importance that it should be protected.[30]

Reducing the threat to East Africa's wildlife proved to be a hopeless undertaking, largely because of competing political and economic interests. In 1959, for example, Kenyan authorities allocated an additional £30,000 to the Game Department to recruit and equip mobile anti-poaching squads for duty in Tsavo National Park. After the Legislative Council approved this budgetary increase, the Department of Forests, Game and Fisheries re-allocated the entire sum to another purpose.[31] In Tanganyika, many wildlife officials believed that penalties for poachers were inadequate, or that cases were dismissed.[32]

The wild dog, which is known as the "wolf of Africa" and which lives in packs of six to forty individuals, preys on duikers, waterbucks, impalas, gazelles, and reedbucks.

Courtesy of Gerald Rilling

30. Quoted in N. Simon, *Between the Sunlight and the Thunder: The Wildlife of Kenya* (Boston: Houghton Mifflin Company, 1963), p. 172.

31. Huxley, Notes on Wildlife, p. 3.

32. *Ibid.*, p. 2.

Nowhere was game preservation more in danger of failing than in Uganda. According to Bruce Kinloch, the greatest threat to the country's fauna was "the pessimism of most of those in high authority, which sprang from a deeply ingrained belief that when Uganda gained independence game reserves would be abolished and all large game animals would be slaughtered."[33] Throughout the last years of British colonial rule, another, more serious menace to Uganda's fauna emerged—overcrowding. In Murchison Falls National Park, overcrowding started turning the habitat into a desert. Elephant herds killed thousands of trees by eating their bark, thus initiating a process whereby forest and acacia woodland were turned into open savanna. To find food, the elephants resorted to shamba raiding.[34]

The other overcrowding issue concerned the proliferation of hippopotamuses in Queen Elizabeth National Park. The massive beasts, which normally spend the day wallowing in shallow water, feed at night on surrounding grasslands. Because of the relatively safe and fertile environment in the Lake Edward and Lake George regions adjacent to the park, the hippopotamus population, which soared to an estimated 14,000, quickly denuded feeding areas of all vegetation.[35] Under the Fulbright Scholarship Program's auspices, two American scientists—George Petrides, Professor of Wildlife Management at Michigan State University and Dr. Wendell Swank, Director of Research, Arizona Game and Fish Department—studied this problem. In their report to the Uganda National Parks Board of Trustees, they noted that the park's establishment had reduced hunting to such an extent that a population explosion was inevitable. As a result, the park's grass cover all but disappeared, enabling gully and sheet erosion to spread over the bare, exposed earth.[36]

Petrides and Swank believed the Board of Trustees could wait for nature to resolve the problem by starvation and disease, in which case the park animals and several other species might be damaged permanently. There also was the danger that anthrax, which was endemic among the region's hippopotamuses, would become a threat to humans and domestic livestock. Since the Americans believed that the risks of a do nothing policy far outweighed any potential gains, they recommended that the Board of Trustees take steps to reduce the hippopotamus population by 50 percent.[37]

---

33. B. Kinloch, *The Shamba Raiders* (London: Collins and Harvill Press, 1972), p. 223.

34. Ibid., p. 327. Also, see Uganda National Parks, *Report and Accounts of the Trustees of the Uganda National Parks 1959* (Kampala: Uganda National Parks, 1960), pp. 9-12.

35. Kinloch, *Shamba Raiders*, pp. 328-29.

36. Ibid., pp. 327-28. Also, see Uganda National Parks, *Report and Accounts of the Trustees of the Uganda National Parks 1957* (Kampala: Uganda National Parks, 1958), pp. 19-20.

37. Uganda National Parks, *Report and Accounts of the Trustees of the Uganda National Parks 1958* (Kampala: Uganda National Parks, 1959), p. 10.

To many trustees, especially those who had devoted their lives to preserving wildlife, this was sheer nonsense. Rennie Bere, the National Parks' Director, led those opposed to the Petrides-Swank solution. In Bere's opinion, there would be an international outcry if the trustees accepted such a harsh remedy, that an extermination policy would be the park's "death knell," and that he, Bere, would resign rather than preside over the destruction of thousands of hippopotamuses. Bruce Kinloch and his followers, on the other hand, said adoption of a cropping scheme would be "the first exercise in positive wildlife management in any national park on the African continent." To end this impasse, Ralph Dreschfield, chairman of the Board of Trustees, solicited the opinions of wildlife organizations and experts throughout the world. With few exceptions, the responses supported the Petrides-Swank findings.[38]

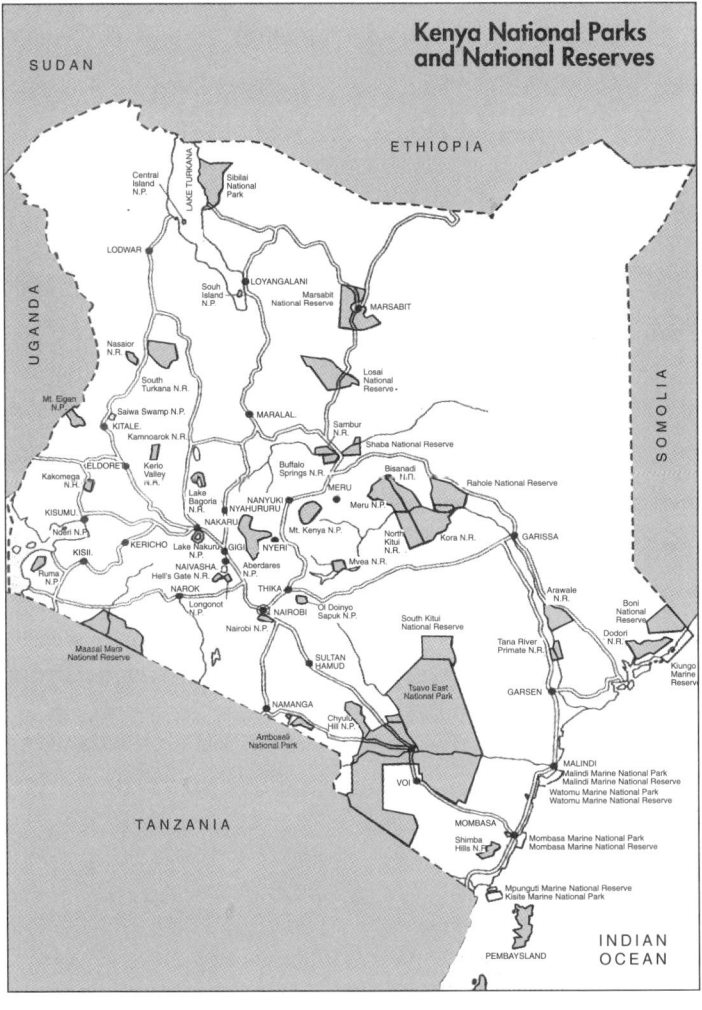

---

38. Kinloch, *Shamba Raiders*, pp. 329-30. In all fairness, it should be pointed out that, during an interview with this author, Bere claimed Kinloch's account was overly dramatic.

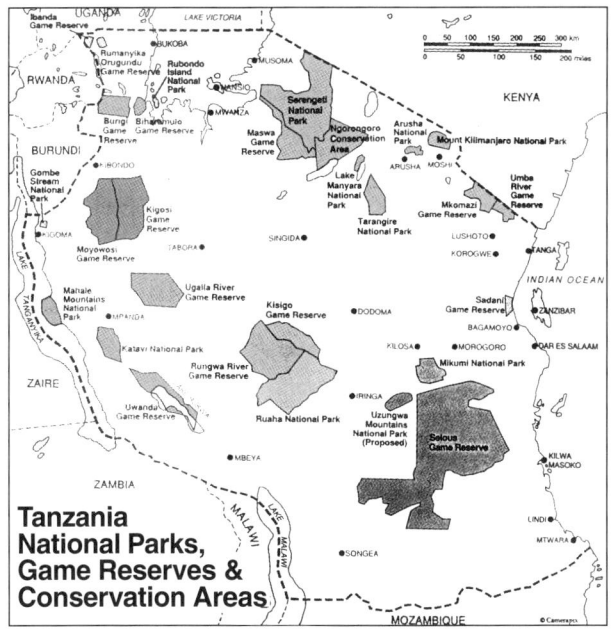

The Board of Trustees therefore approved a reduction experiment on the Mweya Peninsula and in the Kirorongo-Katunguru Wallow Area. Robin D. Fairrie—a Game Department officer who did almost all the shooting—killed approximately 500 hippopotamuses during May and June 1958. The project was a complete success. Officials gave away some meat and sold the rest to the local population, using the proceeds to help run the park. Within two years, grass cover on the Mweya Peninsula and elsewhere in the park matured. This, in turn, enabled species like the kob, waterbuck, buffalo, and elephant to repopulate previously abandoned regions of Queen Elizabeth National Park.[39]

On a broader level, animal cropping, which soon became popular throughout East Africa, exposed the limitations of national parks. Indeed, most conservationists realized that, however well-intentioned, national parks were artificial creations capable of supporting only a limited number of wild animals. Unchecked population increases or drastic food supply reductions from drought or other natural disasters could endanger not only a park's existence but also all fauna within its boundaries. Seen in this light, a national park was nothing more than a fragile refuge, subject to all the pressures of an encroaching civilization. As East Africa's wild areas were turned into farms, towns, and cities to satisfy the demands of a rapidly expanding human society, more and more animals were forced into national parks. When a particular park's animal population reached a critical point, authorities had to eliminate the excess.

---

39. *Ibid.*, p. 330.

CHAPTER V

National Parks: The Reality

By the end of the Second World War, it was evident that game preservation and economic development were incompatible. Indeed, because of the need to improve East Africa's standard of living, there appeared to be little prospect of the region's fauna surviving the twentieth century. To make matters worse, the game departments—whose activities were severely curtailed during the war—were hopelessly understaffed and under-financed, and unable to police adequately the vast territories within their care. In addition, the demand for land for every purpose, agricultural, pastoral, or industrial, African or European, continued to increase, causing pressure to develop in areas hitherto regarded as wildlife sanctuaries. Medical and veterinary officers in each of the three territories also contributed to the case against fauna by voicing concern about the role they played in the transmission of diseases.

In this atmosphere, effective wildlife preservation required a revolutionary policy that struck a balance between the forces of social and economic development and those of nature. Since the 1920s, scores of wildlife enthusiasts—led by Archie Ritchie, Charles Pitman, and Charles Swynnerton—believed this could be accomplished by establishing a national park system throughout East Africa. Unlike ordinary reserves, a national park's territorial integrity was inviolable, and could only be changed by the appropriate legislative authority rather than by mere administrative decision. Conservationists the world over hoped that national parks would provide permanent and absolute protection for wild animals.

One of the first steps to create such a system occurred on 5 March 1930, when the Fauna Preservation Society sent a delegation to the Colonial Office to meet with the Secretary of State for the Colonies, Lord Passfield (Sidney Webb). The Earl of Onslow, head of the group and a wildlife enthusiast, opened the session by noting there was a general pro-wildlife consensus in the empire regarding game preservation. He also said the Fauna Preservation Society "fully recognized that the development of civilization in East Africa should not be imperilled by an undue regard for the preservation of wild and destructive game." He suggested that a joint conference of East African Game Wardens discuss the possibility of adopting a common policy to preserve as much fauna as possible. Such a conference also could discuss the possibility of formulating a national parks contingency plan which would indicate when and where such parks could be established.[1]

Although Passfield was in sympathy with the Fauna Preservation Society, he rejected the Game Wardens' conference idea, pointing out that a similar meeting had been held in 1927, and its recommendations had been forwarded to the appropriate government agencies. Moreover, if the British government convened another conference, it undoubtedly would interrupt the normal activities of the respective game departments. Passfield also believed that differing local conditions made a common policy impossible, and that the colonial governments, rather than game departments, should determine when and where national parks could be created. He mentioned, however, that if the Closer Union scheme—which sought the federation of Kenya, Uganda, and Tanganyika—became a reality, the British government probably would appoint a High Commissioner who could formulate a uniform game policy which would take local circumstance into account.[2] As an alternative to a Game Wardens' conference, Passfield suggested that the Fauna Preservation Society send a representative to East Africa to study the situation and then submit recommended policy changes to the British government. The Earl of Onslow agreed, telling Passfield that he "hoped that it would be sympathetically considered in the Colonial Office together with the other recommendations made by the Deputation."[3]

On 23 May 1930, the Fauna Preservation Society dispatched Major R.W.G. Hingston—their African delegate who had spent many years hunting in India—to Northern Rhodesia, Nyasaland, Tanganyika, Kenya, and Uganda "to discuss with the Governors, Game Wardens, and other interested persons the future policy regarding wildlife."[4] After a five-month tour, Hingston returned to England hoping to change game preservation concepts throughout eastern Africa. On 6 November, in *East Africa*, a London-based newspaper, he stated, "that the construction and development of National Parks. . .would attract great numbers of visitors and prove not only of instruction and interest to them but of real economic value to the Colonies concerned."[5]

Approximately five weeks later, Hingston published an article, "Plea for National Parks," in the *Illustrated London News*. He included photographs obviously designed to

---

1. "Joint Deputation to H.M. Secretary of State for the Colonies," *Journal of the Society for the Preservation of the Empire*, New Series Part XI (1930), pp. 11-3.

2. *Ibid.*, pp. 14-5.

3. A.B. Acheson, undated minute probably written during the early 1930s contained in CO 822/34.

4. R.W.G. Hingston, "Proposed British National Parks for Africa," *Geographical Journal*, Vol. LXXVII No. 5 (May, 1931), p. 1.

5. *East Africa*, 6 November 1930, p. 254.

gain the reader's sympathy, and criticized the British government's efforts to preserve East Africa's fauna by a system of game reserves and laws:

> The laws are drawn up carefully and administered conscientiously, but they cannot be regarded as anything but checks; they are brakes, as it were, on the destructive machinery.[6]

On 9 March 1931, Hingston delivered a report about his trip to the Royal Geographical Society, drawing attention to the fact that the "whole African fauna is steadily failing before the forces of destruction brought to bear against it." He believed the only solution to this problem was the complete and permanent separation of man and animal, something ordinary game reserves were unable to accomplish:

> The weak point about the reserve is its insecurity and want of permanency. It is brought into existence by a Proclamation in the local Government Gazette, provided that the Secretary of State agrees. It can be removed by the same easy means. Should at any time a demand arise for a portion or the whole of a game reserve to be allocated to some other purpose, as, for instance, agricultural development, it is not easy for even the Home Government to resist the demand. . .In point of fact the game reserves of Africa are from time to time contracted, abolished, or altered in some way by this type of legislation. It is only a matter of time before a public demand will arise for the reserves or some portion of them to be thrown open, and there is no guarantee that any game reserve in Africa will last over an extended period of time.

Hingtson also said that national parks would possess more permanency and stability because they would be created by an Act of Parliament that could be changed only by a subsequent Act of Parliament. He recommended the establishment of nine national parks, seven to be located in East Africa.[7]

Later that year, in response to Hingston's activities, the British government dispatched a delegation to the International Congress for the Protection of Nature, which was held in Paris, under the auspices of the French Natural History Museum. The Earl of Onslow, His Majesty's official representative, advised the delegates that in the territories for which they were responsible, the British government "regard themselves as trustees for the protection of Nature not only in the interests of their present inhabitants, but in those of the world at large and of future generations." Because of the migratory nature of most species, however,

---

6. R.W.G. Hingston, "Plea for National Parks," *Illustrated London News*, 13 December 1930, p. 1062.

7. Hingston, "Proposed Parks," pp. 406-17; also, see *The Times*, 10 March 1931, p. 7.

Onslow believed that international action was required "to supplement the effects of individual governments." For this reason, Captain Keith Caldwell, the Fauna Preservation Society delegate, proposed to convene an international conference based on the 1900 London Convention to discuss the future of wildlife preservation.[8]

In 1933, the British government therefore invited nations with African colonies or territories to London to attend the Second International Conference for the Protection of the Fauna and Flora of Africa. The conference, chaired by the Earl of Onslow, opened on 31 October, in the Moses Room at the House of Lords.[9]

On 8 November, Egypt, the Union of South Africa, and the European powers with African possessions signed an agreement which remained in force for the next twenty years. The delegates agreed to a precise definition of the term "national park":

> The expression "national park" shall denote an area (a) placed under public control, the boundaries of which shall not be altered or any portion be capable of alienation except by the competent legislative authority; (b) set aside for the propagation, protection, and preservation of wild animal life and wild vegetation, and for the preservation of objects of aesthetic, geological, prehistoric, historical, archaeological, or other scientific interest for the benefit, advantage, and enjoyment of the general public; (c) in which the hunting, killing or capturing of fauna and the destruction or collection of flora is prohibited except by or under the direction or control of the park authorities. In accordance with the above provisions facilities shall, so far as possible, be given to the general public for observing the fauna and flora in national parks.

The convention also directed the delegates to "explore forthwith" the possibility of establishing national parks in their respective territories. Other provisions included regulation of the trophy trade, preservation of endangered species, and prohibition of hunting from automobiles and aircraft.[10]

The British government ratified this document on 9 April 1935, binding Kenya, Uganda, and Tanganyika to its terms. It was not until the post-World War II era, however, that an East African national park system became a reality. The war and numerous other factors prevented the immediate creation of national parks. Overcoming these obstacles marked the beginning of the last British attempt to establish a more stable man-animal relationship.

---

8. "International Congress for the Protection of Nature," *Journal of the Society for the Preservation of the Fauna of the Empire*, New Series Part XV (December, 1931), p. 48.

9. *East Africa*, 2 November 1933, p. 145.

10. Great Britain. *Agreements Concluded at the International Conference for the Protection of the Fauna and Flora of Africa*, Cmd. 4453 (London: HMSO, 1934), pp. 24, 26.

Kenya

Kenya led the national park movement. On 31 July 1930, Sir Edward Grigg, Kenya's Governor, convened a conference at Government House, Nairobi, "to consider outstanding questions relating to game preservation." Attendees included Archie Ritchie; Lord Delamere, who represented the European settler community; and Major R.W.G. Hingston, an unofficial observer. Grigg appointed a subcommittee under Ritchie to investigate "the desirability of establishing a definite National Park as a permanent game sanctuary in the Colony."[11] On 19 September 1930, Ritchie presented recommendations to the standing conference as to where national parks could be located. Sites included the Northern Reserve, the region north of Sabaki River (between the Kamba and Giriama Reserves), and a tract on the Aberdare mountain range northwest of Nairobi. Grigg endorsed Ritchie's report.[12]

Nine months later, Ritchie, in a memorandum to the Commissioner for Local Government, Lands and Settlement, made the first definite proposal for the creation of a national park:

> Nairobi has a priceless and unique possession in the proximity to its centre of one of the most remarkable pieces of game country in the world. Indeed I have not seen nor heard of any area of country so small in extent which contains a variety and abundance of animal life at all comparable to that found in the Nairobi commonage.[13]

Nairobi National Park was Kenya's first national park. Since opening in 1946 the park has attracted visitors from all over the world and has served as an important symbol of Kenya's commitment to wildlife preservation.

Courtesy of Monty Brown

---

11. M. Cowie, History of the Royal National Parks of Kenya, Rhodes House, Oxford, MSS.AFR S398, p. 9.

12. *Ibid.*, p. 10.

13. Ritchie to Commissioner for Local Government, Lands and Settlement, 26 June 1931, quoted in Ibid., pp. 12-3.

During the First World War, the colonial government designated part of the commonage as a military staging area; and, during the late 1930s, the Royal Air Force used another section as a target range.

Numerous cattle-herding Somalis, the majority of retired askaris who had served the British military in the early days of the twentieth century, also lived in the region. Despite the possibility of a clash between wild animals and the Somali herdsmen, the Kenya Land Commission which convened in 1933 to determine the African population's land requirements, supported Ritchie's recommendation.[14]

Kenya Game Department. Game Rangers and Office Staff, Kenya Game Department Headquarters, 1957. Back Row (left to right): Colonel Neil Sandeman, David Brown, Ken Smith, Ian Parker, Ross Howard. Middle Row: David Allen, Jack Barrah, Rodney Elliot, Colonel Roger Hunt, Julian McKeand. Front Row: Dennis Kearry, Coles, Douglas Smith (Fish Warden), William Hale (Chief Game Warden), Major Lyn Temple (c) Boreham.

Subsequently, a controversy developed between Ritchie and the British government over some clauses in the agreement concluded at the 1933 wildlife conference, which postponed the creation of Nairobi's national park for several years. The difficulty started on 17 September 1934, when Ritchie sent an inquiry to the Colonial Office asking about

---

14. *Ibid.*, p. 15.

a national park's legal status. The Secretary of State for the Colonies informed Ritchie that "a National Park does not necessarily mean an area in which an active and possibly expensive policy of development with a view to attracting tourists must be adopted." The Secretary also told Ritchie that "a National Park is not an area in which hunting by members of the public must be entirely prohibited."[15]

Mervyn Cowie, first director of the Royal National Parks of Kenya, claimed the Colonial Office scheme offered the animals "far less security than they had within the existing and unsatisfactory system of game reserves."[16] In view of the Secretary's interpretation, there was "a lull in the enthusiasm of those who had been actively striving to establish National Parks."[17] The movement received another blow at the end of 1936, when Ritchie went to Malaya to help reorganize that country's Game Department.[18]

The following year, Acting Game Warden F.H. Clarke appointed Cowie Honorary Game Warden. Cowie used this position to attack the colonial administration's wildlife policy and mobilize public opinion against the British government's attitude toward national parks. His first significant achievement came on 21 May 1938, when he helped persuade Nairobi's Municipal Council to limit the number of Somali-owned cattle on the commonage to eight hundred to reduce competition for the area's scarce resources. However, the colonial administration lacked sufficient personnel to enforce this decision, and the Somalis continued to graze their herds, which numbered in the thousands, across the rapidly deteriorating landscape. During the next several months Cowie spoke to many individuals and organizations about the necessity of preserving Kenya's wildlife. Although almost everyone was sympathetic and encouraging, Cowie failed to make any progress toward the establishment of a national park system.[19]

Archie Ritchie. A.T.A. Ritchie was one of East Africa's earliest advocates of a national park system.

Courtesy of Monty Brown

Following Ritchie's return from Malaya in August 1938, Cowie launched an all-out campaign aimed at "provoking public opinion into such a state of enthusiasm" that the colonial administration would be forced

---

15. *Ibid.*, p. 17.

16. M. Cowie, *I Walk with Lions* (New York: The Macmillan Company, 1961), p. 73.

17. Cowie, History of the Royal Parks, p. 18; also, Cowie, *Walk With Lions*, p. 73.

18. Cowie, History of the Royal Parks, p. 18.

19. *Ibid.*, pp. 20, 74-5; also, Cowie, *Walk with Lions*, p. 76.

to address the national park issue.[20] Cowie started feeding a small pride of lions in the Kesserian Valley near Nairobi, knowing they would remain in the region as long as the handouts continued. On several occasions he brought wildlife antagonists to this "hidden" game reserve to observe this.

This tactic often transformed opponents into supporters, or caused them to withhold their objections and reconsider the wildlife problem. Sir Robert Brooke-Popham, Kenya's Governor from 1937 to 1940, was one of the more influential Kesserian Valley visitors. After seeing the lions and being charged by an old rhinoceros, the breathless governor, according to Cowie, "was full of praise, and asked how a scheme could be promoted to enable visitors from overseas to enjoy the same exciting afternoon which he had experienced."[21] Cowie used this opportunity to explain the advantages of a national park system. Despite these successes, the overall situation remained largely unchanged and, at the beginning of 1939, Cowie adopted a more unorthodox strategy to attract public attention. With the assistance of George Kinnear, editor of the widely-circulated *East African Standard*, an avalanche of pro-wildlife "planted" letters—drafted by Cowie but signed by others—poured into the newspaper's Nairobi office from all over Kenya.[22] Cowie himself started the campaign with an emotional appeal to the newspaper's readers:

> The insecurity and conflict of interests resulting from the present system of Game Reserves in Kenya urges me with utmost sincerity to appeal for support through your columns from anyone who really has the interests of Kenya at hand and who shares my belief that game can be made to play an increasingly important part in the necessary development of 'Britain's most attractive colony.'[23]

Over the next several weeks, scores of letters examined the national park question from every possible point of view. On 13 February 1939, for example, an enraged "subscriber" claimed that Kenya's game situation is "now adrift among the rocks of difficulty most of which have been deliberately dropped in the fairway of progress by lazy and selfish officialdom."[24] Two days later, Eliot Tarlton of Nairobi argued for a commonage free "from

---

20. Cowie, History of the Royal Parks, p. 20.

21. For an amusing description of this tactic, see Cowie, *Walk with Lions*, pp. 87-115.

22. It is interesting to note that in *Walk with Lions*, p. 79, Cowie maintains that the campaign was spontaneous, while in the unpublished History of the Royal Parks, he claims the letter crusade was a contrived publicity stunt.

23. *EAS*, 10 February 1939, p. 9.

24. *EAS*, 13 February 1939, p. 7.

native cattle and R.A.F. bombs."[25] Another "reader" maintained that the very idea of a national park on the commonage "must appeal as a sound business proposition—a gold mine on the steps of our capital."[26] Cowie's publicity campaign reached its apex during the week of 17 February, when the East African Standard printed seventeen letters and an editorial favorable to the establishment of a national park system.[27]

During the second half of February, Cowie waited for an official response, but, aside from the Nairobi District Council's decision to "associate itself" with calls for a national park on the commonage, nothing happened. Indeed, officialdom "was singularly silent and apparently disinterested."[28] In despair, Cowie resorted to reverse psychology, and wrote one last letter to the *East African Standard* under the *nom-de-plume* "Old Settler," advocating the total destruction of Kenya's wildlife:

> How can any progress be made in a new farming country unless the danger and damage by game is removed? What was the object of keeping thousands of useless creatures merely to eat all the grass which cattle should have, or to spoil crops or kill livestock. Better to rid the land of all this nonsense. Put the army on to destroying them with machine guns; it would be good training practice. Destroy the females so that they could breed no more. Put down poison for all the predators.[29]

Much to Cowie's consternation the scheme initially backfired when the Nanyuki Farmer's Association, already on record as favoring wildlife extermination on private land, supported his plan.[30] To extricate himself from this predicament, Cowie, with the Nairobi Rotary Club's support, planned to convene a public meeting at the Playhouse Theater preceded by a free showing of some color nature films. Cowie intended to put forward a national park resolution, which immediately would be seconded by Major Jack Riddell, an ardent conservationist who served in the Legislative Council as the elected member for Kiambu. Riddell fell ill and was unable to attend the meeting, so Cowie approached Mervyn Hill, at the time an *East African Standard* staff writer, and persuaded him to replace Riddell.

---

25. *EAS*, 15 February 1939, p. 9. As mentioned earlier, the RAF used part of the commonage for target practice during the late 1930s.

26. *EAS*, 17 February 1939, p. 9.

27. The breakdown is as follows: *EAS*, 20 February 1939, p. 7, four letters; *EAS*, 22 February 1939, p. 9, two letters; *EAS*, 24 February 1939, pp. 7, 22, eight letters. The last issue also carried an editorial entitled "Destruction of Game," p. 4.

28. *EAS*, 27 February 1939, p. 5; also, see Cowie, Walk with Lions, p. 79.

29. Cowie, *Walk with Lions*, pp. 79-80.

30. *Ibid.*, p. 80; also, see *EAS* 24 February 1939, p. 4.

The meeting was finally held on 6 March 1939, before a standing-room-only crowd of approximately 700 settlers, officials, and spectators. Even Riddell got up from his sick bed to attend. The films were a success and the audience—which Cowie claimed was "the final straw which broke the sluggish Government camel's back"—unanimously passed the following resolution:

> Be it resolved that this meeting emphasizes the public demand, not only
> for the establishment of National Game Parks in Kenya, but for adequate
> Game Control, and protests against any further delay in the formation of
> a properly constituted National Trust for the preservation of the Colony's
> invaluable assets—its fauna and flora.[31]

The colonial administration responded on 28 April 1939, by appointing the Game Policy Committee, with Cecil Hoey, a settler and former big game hunter, as chairman. Hoey was instructed to make recommendations "concerning the institution in the Colony of a National Game Park or Parks, including their location, extent, constitution, control and management."[32] Unfortunately, the committee had to postpone its activities temporarily at the end of August 1940, because of the war.

By early 1942, however, the Game Policy Committee resumed limited operations and, after hearing evidence from representatives of the Nairobi Chamber of Commerce, the Kenya Association, the Stock Breeder's Association, and a host of government agencies, recommended that the commonage be made into a national park. It also urged that each Somali family be limited to a maximum of twenty head of cattle and twenty-three sheep; that the military cease activities within the park's boundaries after the war; and that a Board of Trustees be created to administer and protect all national parks.[33]

On 28 January 1945, Kenya's Governor, Sir Philip Mitchell, approved "An Ordinance to Provide for the Establishment of National Parks and for the Preservation of Wild Animal Life." The regulation stipulated that "The Governor may, with the consent of the Legislative Council of the Colony, by Proclamation in the *Gazette*, declare any area of land to be a National Park." For land in the "White Highlands" region of southwestern Kenya, the Governor had to consult first with the Highlands Board; and, in the case of African reserves and leasehold regions, he worked through the Trust Board. Once created, national parks could be altered only with the approval of the Governor, Legislative Council, Board

---

31. Cowie, History of the Royal Parks, p. 25; also, see Cowie *Walk with Lions*, pp. 50, 82-3.

32. Colony and Protectorate of Kenya, *Interim Report of the Game Policy Committee* (Nairobi: The Government Printer, 1942), p. 1.

33. For a complete list of the committee's recommendations, see *Ibid.*, pp. 12-4.

of Trustees, and by proclamation in the *Official Gazette*. The ordinance also created a fourteen-member Board of Trustees known as "The Kenya National Parks Trustees."[34]

In the early years of the twentieth century, the Uganda Game Department concentrated its efforts on controlling marauding elephants.

Courtesy of the author

Encouraged by Mitchell's action, the Game Policy Committee issued a Second Interim Report on 14 September 1945, calling for additional national parks in the Sabaki-Tsavo region of southern Kenya and in parts of the Mount Kenya and Aberdare forest reserves. The committee also suggested that "park adjuncts" (viz., areas that could not be considered for national park status because of "existent human rights"), later called national reserves, be established in Ngong Hills near the Nairobi commonage; the Amboseli region adjacent to Mount Kilimanjaro; the Trans-Mara zone bordering on Tanganyika; the western foothills of the Chyulu range in southeastern Kenya; and the land around Marsabit in the Northern Frontier Province.[35] Mitchell welcomed these proposals and, at the Board of Trustees' inaugural meeting on 15 October 1945, exhorted the delegates to perform their duties with courage, determination, and conviction:

---

34. *Ibid.*, pp. 2, 10. A copy of the ordinance is contained in the *Journal of the Society for the Preservation of the Fauna of the Empire*, New Series Part LI (May, 1945), pp. 10-4.

35. Colony and Protectorate of Kenya, *Second Interim Report of the Game Policy Committee* (Nairobi: The Government Printer, 1945), pp. 2-6.

I feel that we can look forward to steady progress and I hope, to the fairly rapid development of the enormously valuable asset which our National Park's will certainly be. In wishing God-speed in your important tasks I will add only this, that I am convinced that a project such as the establishment of National Parks is not worth undertaking unless it is undertaken boldly and with imagination. . .We have an opportunity of developing an asset of the greatest value to our country. . .the preservation for posterity of all that is interesting and beautiful in wild nature.[36]

Mitchell's support facilitated the administrative process, and, on 16 December 1946, the colonial government gazetted the forty-four-square-mile Nairobi Park; on 2 April 1948, the 8,024-square-mile Tsavo National Park; on 6 December 1949, the 240- square-mile Mount Kenya National Park, and on 19 May 1950, the Aberdares National Park.[37]

Thus, within six years of their appointment, the trustees had established national parks in all regions recommended by the Game Policy Committee. Cowie claimed these parks had two functions:

The first duty is clearly to preserve and safeguard all objects within a national park...and as far as possible, to ensure that the places forming that trust will remain unimpaired for the benefit of future generations. Our second main duty is to develop our national parks for the interest, advantage and enjoyment of the public.[38]

Until the end of British colonial rule in 1963, Cowie, the trustees, and thousands of private supporters throughout the world struggled to achieve these goals.

Uganda

Next to elephant preservation, poaching was the biggest problem confronting Uganda after the Second World War. Indeed, according to the Game Department, "by early 1946 even the best-stocked areas were wearing thin."[39] Poaching was popular because of the exorbitant cost of meat and ivory. As late as 1959, the country's annual per capita income varied between a low of 11 shillings in Ankole to a high of 174 shillings in Buganda. An

---

36. Royal National Parks of Kenya, *Report 1946-50* (Nairobi: Royal National Parks of Kenya, 1951), p. 8.

37. Ironically, Mitchell fails to mention the national park issue in his memoirs, *African Afterthoughts* (London: Hutchinson, 1954).

38. Royal National Parks of Kenya, *Report 1946-50*, p. 1.

39. Uganda Protectorate, *Annual Report Game Department 1948* (Entebbe: Government Printer, 1949), p. 4.

The elusive leopard often seeks refuge in the tree tops.

Courtesy of Gerald Rilling

African poacher could earn as much as 200 shillings for selling the meat of one buffalo or eland; 100 to 400 shillings for a pair of elephant tusks; or 150 shillings for a leopard skin. [40]

Efforts to end this illicit business were nearly always ineffective and sometimes dangerous. For example, a "notorious poacher" killed a Game Guard in the Siba forest near the Waki River in Bunyoro. The murderer escaped, causing Pitman to conclude:

> It must be recorded to the undying shame of the people of Bunyoro. . .that they are willing to protect a cold-blooded and brutal murderer as long as he will provide them with free or cheap meat from the animals he poaches.[41]

The creation of manageable, easily policed national parks that were of little or no value to African or European agriculturists obviously would help solve these problems. In addition, national parks would protect wild animals from the "ambitious schemes of the

40. Uganda Protectorate, *Annual Report Game Department 1950* (Entebbe: Government Printer, 1951), p. 5; also, see R.M.A. van Zwanenberg with Anne King, *An Economic History of Kenya and Uganda 1800-1970* (London: Macmillan Press Ltd., 1977), p. 71.

41. Uganda Protectorte, *Annual Report Game Department 1950*, p. 61.

post-war development planners [which] took no account of the effect on wildlife of their despoliation of the natural environment."[42] Unfortunately, the worldwide economic depression and the fact that ungulates like the buffalo carried rinderpest, the dreaded cattle disease, hampered Pitman's plans.

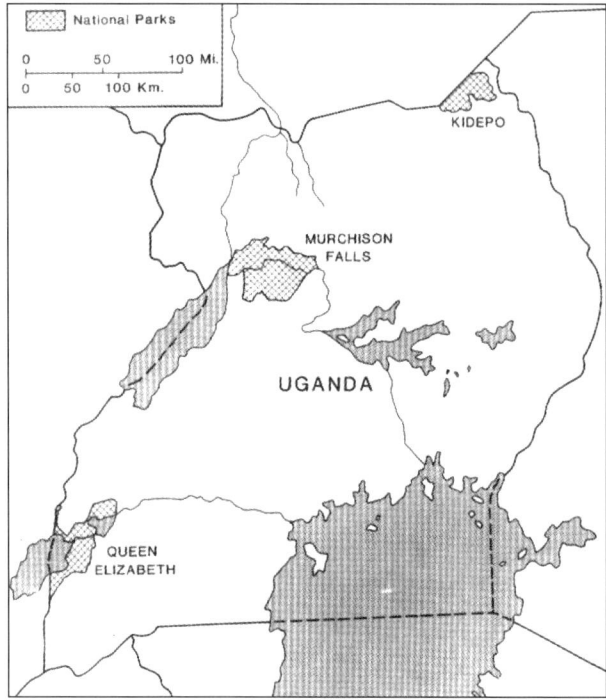

After the Second World War, however, the increasing diminution of Uganda's wildlife gradually overshadowed these considerations. In 1947, Dr. Barton Worthington, author of the country's development plan and a noted conservationist, included £16,600 in the government's budget for national parks. Then, on 20 December 1948, the colonial administration created the Uganda National Parks Committee "to consider and make recommendations concerning the institution in Uganda of a National Park or Parks, including their location, extent, constitution, control and management." After four meetings, during which there was a "general lack of response from the public," the committee issued its final report, which recommended the establishment of national parks in Ruwenzori, Katwe, Murchison Falls, and in the Virunga mountains.

Before accepting the report, the colonial administration solicited the comments of Pitman's successor, Bruce Kinloch, an authority on the African elephant. He submitted a

---

42. C.R.S. Pitman, Evidence given to the Tsetse Fly Sub-committee, 1 January 1931, CAB 58/51; also, see B. Kinloch, *The Shamba Raiders* (London: Collins and Haverhill, 1972), p. 206.

highly critical memorandum to Uganda's Chief Secretary on 21 May 1951, admonishing the committee for suggesting that less than 10 percent of Uganda's existing game reserves should be granted national park status. Moreover, Kinloch pointed out that most wild animals were great wanderers and could not be kept on a "postage stamp," especially in view of the fact that extensive mineral and agricultural development threatened the Katwe region. Kinloch was also pessimistic about the Murchison Falls proposal since the Acholi Council was opposed to national parks. He observed that if the colonial administration did not act quickly, Uganda would be the only big game territory in Africa without national parks.[43]

There was little else Kinloch could do as he was then in England on home leave. Back in Uganda, however, Acting Game Warden John Mills continued the struggle for the creation of a national park system. He discovered a useful ally in Sir George Cartland, the Secretariat's Administrative Secretary. Cartland arranged for the secondment of Ken Beaton, Warden of Nairobi National Park, to visit Uganda and advise the colonial administration about the suitability of the regions the Uganda National Parks Committee had recommended as national parks.

Beaton, an ex-settler/ farmer who had the reputation of being able to charm a spitting cobra, arrived in Uganda near the end of October 1951, and spent three weeks touring game areas in Ankole, Toro, Bunyoro, Acholi, West Nile, and Karamoja. He also interviewed numerous people. After this fact-finding mission, Beaton sent a report to the colonial administration urging the creation of two national parks. The first, to be known as Murchison Falls National Park, was in the Victoria Nile vicinity, and encompassed about 1,500 square miles. The other, initially called Kazinga but later changed to Queen Elizabeth, was located about 300 miles south of Murchison Falls between Lakes Edward and George and was approximately 700 square miles.[44]

Meanwhile, in late September 1951, Charles Pitman, then retired, told Kinloch, still on home leave, that Sir Andrew Cohen was slated to replace Sir John Hall as Governor of Uganda. Kinloch telephoned the Colonial Office and requested an interview with Cohen, at that time serving as Under-Secretary of State and head of the African Division. Cohen promised Kinloch to "look into the [national park] matter directly [after] I arrive [in Uganda]."[45]

---

43. Kinloch to Chief Secretary, 21 May 1951, contained in Kinloch, *Shamba Raiders*, pp. 288-90.

44. C. Willock, *The Enormous Zoo* (New York: Harcourt, Brace and World Inc., 1964), pp. 7-8; also, see Uganda Protectorte, *Annual Report Game Department* (Entebbe: Government Printer, 1952), p. 14.

45. Kinloch, *Shamba Raiders*, p. 294.

Three days after getting to Entebbe in January 1952, Cohen scheduled another interview with Kinloch to discuss local opposition to national parks, a troublesome issue since the late 1940s. Most Africans believed national parks were "an imperialist trick" designed "to take land away from the people."[46] Fortunately, the situation in the proposed Queen Elizabeth National Park region had improved somewhat, enabling Kinloch to inform Sir Andrew that:

> The Omukama of Toro seems to be much less hostile than he was to the
> prospect of a national park in the area of Lakes George and Edward, and
> the Omugabe of Ankole appears to have become reconciled to the idea
> that the park should extend into his kingdom.[47]

Kinloch also pointed out that the major problem confronting the proposed Queen Elizabeth National Park concerned the Agriculture Department's long-term land-use plans. According to a Department spokesman, local inhabitants around Lakes Edward and George were reluctant to have any cotton-producing land included in a national park. Sir Andrew welcomed the news about Toro and Ankole and blandly asserted that he was confident that the Director of Agriculture could allay the suspicions of African land owners.[48]

After listening to Kinloch's report, Cohen said:

> I am convinced that Uganda must have national parks and I agree
> with you that if we have them at all they must be large enough to be
> worth while. If necessary, I intend to force this matter through the
> Legislative Council. I shall ask the Attorney General to go ahead
> with drafting appropriate legislation, for which he will need your
> advice. In the meantime I want you to get these boundary questions
> settled as quickly as possible.[49]

Despite the governor's support for national parks, pockets of resistance persisted. Like the Acholi Council, the Uganda National Congress—founded in 1952 as the first nationwide African political party—believed national parks were ruses to take land away from Africans. It, therefore, petitioned the British government and then the Labour opposition to stop the establishment of a national park system. When these tactics failed the Congress encouraged the African press to take up the banner against the colonial administration.

---

46. R. Bere, The Story of Uganda National Parks, unpublished manuscript in author's possession, pp. 6, 17-8.

47. Kinloch, *Shamba Raiders*, p. 294.

48. *Ibid.*, pp. 294-5.

49. Kinloch, *Shamba Raiders*, pp. 295-6.

Ken Beaton defused this situation by inviting a group of African newspaper editors to visit Ruwenzori as government guests. He told them:

> It has caused me great distress to see national parks used as a political platform for there is nothing political about national parks. They belong to the people and cannot be taken away. In years to come you will be grateful for the farsightedness of those who fought to preserve these sanctuaries. You will be proud of them, and they will become treasured economic assets. There are national parks all over the world. Just before coming to Uganda I was asked by the Ethiopian government to advise them and suggest ways of setting up a national parks organization. Ethiopia is not controlled by European influences. National Parks are an ideal. The hills, lakes, plains and the wonderful wild creatures were created by God. These are things you should help to preserve for yourselves, your children and your children's children. No one is being deprived of land. Millions of acres outside the parks are lying undeveloped and unused. . .I appeal to your sense of fairness and justice not to bring the national parks into politics.[50]

Beaton's strategy worked, press opposition to the parks stopped, and the way was opened for national parks.

On 28 March 1952, Attorney General Ralph Dreschfield introduced the National Parks Bill in the Legislative Council. To allay any lingering suspicions in the African community, Dreschfield reiterated the government's position that "when a national park is declared it is not taking land from the people," but preserving it for the people for all time. He also pointed out the parks' potential economic benefit to Uganda by drawing attention to the fact that, in 1950, the Royal National Parks of Kenya generated £3 million in revenue.[51]

During the debate, several Africans criticized the proposed legislation. B.J. Mukasa argued for majority African representation on the Board of Trustees, while P.C. Ofwono claimed the bill failed to "allow for consultation with Local Authorities."[52] Dreschfield responded that at least two African members, and possibly more, would be on the Board of Trustees. He also agreed to move an amendment permitting the governor to declare a national park after consultation with local African authorities in which the area is located .[53]

---

50. Interview, Rene Bere; Bere, Story of Uganda National Parks, pp. 6, 17-8. For the Uganda National Congress's position, see S.R. Karugire, *A Political History of Uganda* (Nairobi: Heinemann, 1980), p. 149.

51. Uganda Protectorate, *Legislative Council Proceedings, 28 March 1952* (Entebbe: Government Printer, 1952), p. 40.

52. *Ibid.*, p. 42.

53. *Ibid.*, pp. 45-6; also, see Uganda National Parks, *Report and Accounts of the Trustees of the Uganda National Parks 1952* (Kampala: Uganda National Parks, 1953), p. 1.

With these matters resolved, the bill passed its second reading, and, on 3 April, the Legislative Council approved the National Parks Ordinance of Uganda. On 24 July, the colonial administration gazetted Uganda's first two national parks. The Queen Elizabeth National Park was 764 square miles, or about the size of England's Westmoreland county, while Murchison Falls National Park was almost twice as large, or 1,504 square miles.

Although the creation of a national park system was a major breakthrough for wildlife enthusiasts, it was not the end of Uganda's ecological problems. Marauding elephants continued to ravage the country's crops. In addition, growing pressure from agricultural development and African poaching threatened to outweigh the aesthetic, educational, and economic advantages of wild animals.

Tanganyika

Despite Charles Swynnerton's efforts to prove that destruction of wildlife would not stop the spread of sleeping sickness and nagana, the slaughter of Tanganyika's wild animals continued at an alarming rate. In 1948, Captain Keith Caldwell accused a succession of administrations of fostering a "general anti-game mentality," and, even as late as 1965, George Rushby, Tanganyika's Deputy Game Warden, lamented that the country "never had a governor, a chief secretary or any other high administrative official who was in the least game minded."[54] Such lethargy delayed the establishment of a national park system.

No where was the national park issue more explosive than in the 6,000 square-mile Serengeti region of northwestern Tanganyika. As early as 1928, General L.B. Boyd Moss, an influential European settler, had warned the Legislative Council that the government's lackadaisical attitude toward Serengeti could have disastrous ecological, political, and economic repercussions. Sixteen months later, Andries Pienaar, a Moshi resident, wrote to the *East African Standard* criticizing big game hunters who had used motorcars to run down animals before shooting them. He also reported that an American hunter had suggested to his colleagues that they engage in a twenty-four-hour killing spree to see what bag was possible in a single day! On 3 July 1929, Denys Finch-Hatton, a big game hunter and conservationist, sent a letter to *The Times* drawing attention to the Serengeti situation, Pienaar's accusations, and the colonial administration's inability or unwillingness to do anything.[55]

---

54. K. Caldwell, *Report on a Fauna Survey in Eastern and Central Africa* (London: Society for the Preservation of the Fauna of the Empire, Occasional Paper #8, 1948), p. 9.

55. Tanganyika Territory, *Proceedings of the Legislative Council, 17 January 1928*, (Dar es Salaam: Government Printer, 1928), p. 78; EAS, 15 May 1929, p. 11; The Times, 3 July 1929, p. 17.

Over the next few weeks, letters poured into *The Times* expressing outrage at hunters who used unsportsmanlike tactics. Even Douglas Jardine, Chief Secretary to the Government of Tanganyika, railed against hunters who crossed into Serengeti from Kenya "in swift, and sometime armoured motor-cars. . .to massacre lion and buffalo and other game by the score."[56] The public outcry reached a crescendo on 18 July 1929, when *The Times* quoted the Prince of Wales: "Record heads do not mean very much to me; while the idea of going out in a motor-car to massacre game at close quarters—well, I don't care for that at all."[57] When the Serengeti problem came before the House of Commons, a government spokesman assured everyone that "the Government of Tanganyika had already been asked for a report on the matter."

On 26 August 1929, Sir Donald Cameron, Tanganyika's Governor, submitted a memorandum on the subject to the Colonial Office. He pointed out that he already had approved a plan to limit the number of lions to be shot on license in certain Serengeti districts and stationed a Game Ranger "with adequate transport" along the Kenya-Tanganyika border to deter hunters from using motorcars. He also reported that the Attorney General was drafting legislation to prohibit hunting in many areas, increase the penalty for lawbreakers to imprisonment without the option of paying a fine, confiscate any motorcar used to run down animals, and reduce the number of lions on a visitor's license from five to two in the Serengeti.[58]

Despite these measures, international criticism of the governor continued. On 16 October 1930, Arthur Loveridge, Associate Curator of Reptiles Amphibians in the Museum of Comparative Zoology at Harvard University, told the London-based newspaper *East Africa* that Cameron was ignoring wholesale game destruction by African and American hunters who acted with "the mentality of Chicago gangsters." Loveridge even criticized Swynnerton for devoting so much time to tsetse fly research. Loveridge then sent a memorandum to the American Committee for International Wild Life Preservation warning that the majority of Tanganyika's Europeans are "either completely indifferent to the idea of preserving the game or [are] arguing for its ruthless extermination."[59] At the end of 1930, largely as a result of this campaign, the colonial administration gazetted the Serengeti Closed Reserve (the equivalent of a Partial Game Reserve). Under this scheme, hunters had to get special permission to shoot in this area; this to satisfy national park advocates

---

56. For a representative sampling, see *The Times*, 8 July 1929, p. 12; 15 July 1929, p. 15; 16 July 1929, p. 17; and 20 July, 1929, p. 8.

57. Quoted in *The Times*, 18 July 1929, p. 15. 58. Cameron to Passfield, 26 August 1929, CO 736/22.

59. *East Africa*, 16 October 1930, p. 137; Loveridge to American Committee, Some Observations on Game Preservation in Tanganyika 1929-1930, p. 8. In author's possession.

who argued that Serengeti's wildlife would be secure only within an inviolable game sanctuary. As Tanganyika was then in the throes of a depression, the colonial administration was unable to allocate funds for a national parks organization.[60]

The enactment of the 1940 Game Ordinance reflected this economic reality. According to the preamble, the bill was supposed to incorporate the provisions of the 1933 International Convention for the Preservation of Fauna and Flora. In other words, the ordinance was to recognize that the creation of sanctuaries, whose boundaries could not be changed or altered except by legislative authority, was the best way to preserve Africa's wildlife. Instead of embracing this principle, however, the regulation allowed Serengeti's administration to remain in the hands of the colonial administration, advised by the Game Department. Given the fact that the Game Department was concerned primarily with animal control rather than animal protection, this arrangement, born of economic necessity, failed to live up to the national park ideal.

The ordinance also failed to strike a more favorable balance between wild animals and the Maasai people who used Serengeti for grazing. Indeed, the colonial administration gave the Maasai assurance that "their rights would not be disturbed without their agreement."[61] To the Maasai, it was sheer folly to live with wild animals in peace and harmony; yet the government pursued just such a policy. Actually, the colonial administration believed that the Maasai, attracted by new water supplies in other areas, would move out of Serengeti. Even if they remained, officials mistakenly believed the Maasai would not conflict with Serengeti's objectives, "for their customary way of life was in harmony with, and not inimical to, the natural fauna."[62]

By the end of the Second World War, influential members of the European settler community had joined wildlife enthusiasts to demand that Serengeti be administered according to the principles set forth in the 1933 International Convention for the Preservation of Fauna and Flora. On 20 April 1948, Major Dutoit, a settler who served in the Legislative Council as the unofficial member for Arusha, made a persuasive argument for a National Parks Ordinance:

> We farmers have been handicapped now. . .for nearly forty years under
> the restrictions of game preservation. . .We cannot farm and have game

---

60. Tanganyika National Parks, *Reports and Accounts of the Board of Trustees* (Arusha: Tanganyika National Parks, 1955), p. 6; also, see *The Times*, 1 July 1933, p. 13.

61. Tanganyika Territory, *The Serengeti National Park Sessional Paper No. 1 1956* (Dar es Salaam: Government Printer, 1956), p. 1.

62. Ibid., p. 1.

or vermin. . .The sooner this Bill can be implemented. . .the better. . .I should hate to see any game killed unnecessarily but a National Park is the place for rare game. Having that, we can bring our visitors to see it and the farmers in their own areas can keep a clean area away from game and vermin.[63]

When the Legislative Council finally enacted a National Park Ordinance later in the year, it placed responsibility for controlling and managing any park on a Board of Trustees. It failed, however, to alter the government's previous policy regarding human entry and residence:

> Nothing in this Ordinance shall affect the rights of His Majesty, his heirs or successors, or the rights of any person in or over any land acquired before the commencement of this Ordinance.[64]

In view of the fact that, as of 1948, some 8,000 Maasai and their livestock—about 150,000 head of cattle and 150,000 small stock—resided in Serengeti, it was unlikely that the Board of Trustees, or any other administrative agency, could fulfill the terms of the 1933 Convention. According to Article IV of the convention, all contracting governments agreed to "The control of all white or native settlements in national parks with a view to ensuring that as little disturbance as possible is occasioned to the natural fauna and flora." [65] The inability to fulfill this commitment not only weakened the national parks organization but also threatened to poison relations between the colonial government and the Maasai.

Between the early 1950s and the twilight of British imperialism in the early 1960s, the land-use conflict intensified at a frightening pace, causing some critics to suggest that European officials were guilty of malfeasance.[66] As will be shown, these accusations took little or no account of the ecological problems confronting East Africa and were, for the most part, based on unwarranted preconceptions. The succeeding chapter, by way of concluding this study, will briefly examine some of the more serious man-animal conflicts that plagued East Africa during the 1950-1963 period and demonstrate the futility of trying to preserve large numbers of wild animals in societies committed to rapid political, economic, and social development.

---

63. Tanganyika Territory, *Proceedings of the Legislative Council, 20 April 1948* (Dar es Salaam: Government Printer, 1948), p. 9.

64. Tanganyika Territory, *Report of the Serengeti Committee of Enquiry, 1957* (Dar es Salaam: Government Printer, 1957), pp. 7-8.

65. Cmd. 4453, p. 26.

66. A. Graham, *Gardeners of Eden* (London: George Allen and Unwin Ltd., 1963), especially chapters III and IV.

CHAPTER VI

Wildlife Preservation in Independent East Africa

Even before independence it was evident that the new leaders of Kenya, Uganda, and Tanganyika favored continuing the national park policy as a vehicle to preserve the region's wild animals. At the 1961 Arusha Conference[1], Julius Nyerere—who eventually became President of Tanzania—informed the delegates that:

> The survival of our wildlife is a matter of grave concern to all of us in Africa. These wild creatures amid the wild places they inhabit are not only important as a source of wonder and inspiration but are an integral part of our natural resources and of our future livelihood and well being. In accepting the trusteeship of our wildlife we solemnly declare that we will do everything in our power to make sure that our children's grand-children will be able to enjoy this rich and precious inheritance.[2]

Nyerere said that accomplishing this goal depended on the availability of specialist knowledge, trained manpower, and adequate financing. He expressed the hope that other nations would cooperate with independent East Africa in this important task.[3]

Despite the commitment and collaboration of several western nations, the advancing forces of modernization continued to play havoc with the region's dwindling wildlife. By the late 1990s, it was obvious that East Africa's independent governments were as helpless as their British predecessors had been in the struggle to strike a harmonious balance between man and animal.

---

1. "A Symposium on the Conservation of Nature and Natural Resources in Modern African States" sponsored by the Commission for Technical Co-operation in Africa South of the Sahara (CCTA) and the International Union for the Conservation of Nature and Natural Resources (IUCN), supported by the United Nations Educational Scientific and Culture Organization (UNESCO) and the Food and Agricultural Organization of the United Nations (FAO), and orga-nized by ICUN, the CCTA's Scientific Council for Africa South of the Sahara, and the Tanganyika Game Department—representing the host government, Tanganyika.

2. N. Simon, "Arusha Conference," *Wild Life* (December, 1961), p. 37.

3. *Ibid.*, p. 37. It is interesting to note that Elspeth Huxley, in a paper given to the East African Academy Second Symposium on 13 June 1964, maintained that "East Africa cannot expect to sit with a begging bowl," waiting for the west to finance its wildlife preservation program. For an analysis of this paper, see *EAS*, 15 June 1964, p. 5.

Kenya

During the last months of British colonial rule, Jomo Kenyatta—who at the time was Prime Minister—told Kenya's House of Representatives that wildlife was one of the country's most valued treasures:

> The burden of responsibility for the protection of animals is the responsibility of us all. You should not say this is Government business, or let the Government do this or the Government do that. This is something that everyone of us ought to be interested in. These animals are a national asset, and as such we must take great care to protect them.[4]

Apart from aesthetic considerations, the country's fauna supported a growing tourist industry, which earned much needed foreign currency. Indeed, according to the *East African Standard*, tourism was the cornerstone of Kenya's economy and its "greatest potential source of revenue."[5] Despite popular support for game preservation, the ecological situation deteriorated steadily, largely because Kenya's human population required more and more land and water to maintain an acceptable standard of living. Infusions of western aid failed to prevent repeated man-animal conflicts.

Friction was particularly intense among the Maasai people who lived in southern Kenya along the Tanganyika border. Five months prior to independence, S.S. Oloitipitip, a Kenya African Democratic Union (KADU) representative, complained that "day and night" game was killing the Maasai and their livestock, and spreading fatal diseases to their cattle.[6] Appeals by Kenyatta and other African leaders to the Maasai to preserve wildlife were largely ineffective.[7] One of the reasons for anti-fauna sentiment in Maasailand and elsewhere was the fact that individuals who had suffered personal injury or financial loss because of the depredations of wild animals found it difficult to collect government compensation. As a result, many African communities not only shot wildlife to protect private property but also to express discontent with the government's preservation policy.[8]

To resolve this problem, Senator G.K. Kipury, who represented the Maasai district of Kajiado, introduced a motion in Kenya's Senate calling on the government to eliminate

---

4. *EAS*, 2 August 1963, p. 5.

5. *EAS*, 24 May 1963, p. 6.

6. *EAS*, 10 July 1963, p. 3.

7. Quoted in *EAS*, 3 February 1964, p. 5.

8. Republic of Kenya, *Game Department Annual Reports 1964 and 1965* (Nairobi: Government Printer, 1967), pp. 12, 15.

all game outside the national parks to prevent loss of life and damage to property. Other influential African politicians—including J.Z. Kase, the KADU representative from Tana River—sided with Kipury by moving similar resolutions in the House of Representatives.[9] Although such activities failed to gain widespread support, L.G. Sagini, Minister for Lands, Game, Fisheries, Water and Natural Resources, believed it was necessary to issue a statement, pointing out that, "Kenya's Government has no intention of realizing its measures for the preservation of the country's wildlife, as any such relaxation would spell its utter destruction".[10]

Staff shortages in the Game Department unit responsible for matters outside the national parks, also hampered wildlife conservation, particularly in controlling poaching, protecting agriculture from game damage, and winning rural support for wildlife projects. By 1967, budgetary constraints had reduced the Department's size by one quarter. Apart from this consideration, several other factors contributed to the diminution of Kenya's fauna.[11]

On 9 May 1963, for example, Major W.G. Raw, chairman of the council of the East African Wildlife Society, warned that wild animals were likely to suffer from breaking up large-scale European farms and plantations in the former White Highlands for African resettlement. During the colonial period, European-owned tracts adjoining forests on the flanks of Mount Kenya and the Aberdares had not posed an ecological threat, largely because most farmers had accepted some depredation. In addition, there was normally a wide pasture strip between crops and forests that cattle and game shared. Moreover, the crops, mainly cereals and pyrethrum, were not a great attraction to forest animals. With the dissolution of these farms, proliferating African small holdings quickly ran up to the forest edge. The crops grown—maize, beans, potatoes, and sweet potatoes—enticed elephant and buffalo herds. As damage increased, more and more Africans demanded the elimination of these hungry marauders. When the Game Department failed to respond adequately, scores of farmers took matters into their own hands, illegally killing thousands of wild animals.[12]

Poaching was the other problem that plagued Kenya's fauna during the post-1963 era. Hunters, alone or in bands, exterminated wildlife to feed themselves and their families or, more importantly, to satisfy the tourist industry's growing demand for animal trophies.

---

9. *EAS*, 18 September 1963, p. 5; *The Times*, 18 September 1963, p. 11; Government of Kenya, The National Assembly. House of Representatives. *Official Report*, Vol. III, Part II (Nairobi: Government Printer, 1964), pp. 3018, 3020, and 3022-23.

10. Quoted in *EAS*, 22 October 1964, p. 5.

11. *EAS*, 17 April 1967, p. 5.

12. *EAS*, 10 May 1963, p. 5. Also, see *The Times*, 10 May 1963, p. 10.

By December 1977, poaching for profit was so common and widespread that President Kenyatta decreed a ban on any further trade in animal parts, including ivory.[13] As a result, Kenya's lucrative curio shops, an estimated 200 in Nairobi and 200 elsewhere in the country, had just three months to get rid of their stock and cease operations.

The following year, after receiving World Bank funding, Kenya created an anti-poaching unit. Its inability to even slow illegal hunting reflected the difficulty of policing national parks with an understaffed and under-financed anti-poaching unit. Although they killed indiscriminately, poachers normally killed animals that fetched a high price on the world market. In 1985, for example, Kenyan authorities reported that the black rhinoceros population had declined over the past two decades from about 20,000 to between 500 and 600. Elephant ivory also continued to pour through Mombasa en route to the Far East where artisans carved it into objects d'art.

By the late 1980s, it was evident that Kenya's fauna was facing extinction. Facing a loss of tourist revenue, a major source of foreign currency earnings, the Kenyan government embarked on a multi-faceted program to save the country's wildlife. On 18 July 1989, to dramatize his concern for Kenya's elephants, President Daniel Arap Moi set fire to twelve tons of poached ivory tusks worth about $3 million; since then, 18 July has been celebrated annually as Elephant Day all over the country.[14] He also took numerous other steps to stop the slaughter of Kenya's wild animals, including the reorganization of the Department of Wildlife Conservation and Management; and the restructuring of The National Parks of Kenya into the Kenya Wildlife Service (under the directorship of Richard Leakey), a parastatal that promised to improve the country's preservation efforts. Additionally, President Moi ordered the country's security forces to shoot poachers on sight and approved the creation of a new wildlife services corporation to promote wildlife preservation.[15]

Throughout the 1990s, Kenyan authorities continued to make progress toward improving the country's fauna preservation policies. Nairobi supported a world-wide ban on ivory trafficking, which came into force in January 1991 and which brought about an almost immediate decline in elephant poaching in Kenya.[16] More importantly, Kenyan

---

13. In view of the fact that much of Kenyatta's immediate family was involved in the poaching business and illegal ivory trade, many foreign newspapers and journals greeted the decree with skepticism.

14. *The Weekly Review*, 28 July 1989, p. 16. Moi's dramatic gesture, which conservationists throughout the world praised, was the first of several highly publicized burnings of wildlife trophies. Two of the more dramatic burnings occurred on 24 January 1990, when government officials set ablaze 350 rhinoceros horns and other game trophies; and on 18 July 1991, when Kenyan Minister for Tourism and Wildlife, Noah Katana Ngala, burned 1,350 elephant tusks.

15. *The Weekly Review*, 1 September 1989, p. 12.

16. *The Weekly Review*, 17 May 1991, p. 36.

security forces restored stability to the country's national parks and game reserves, many of which had become unsafe because of attacks against foreign tourists by poachers and other criminal elements. Additionally, David Western, a noted conservationist who took over the directorship of the Kenya Wildlife Service in 1994, sought to redefine the man-animal relationship so as to give local communities a greater stake in wildlife preservation.[17]

Although conservationists throughout the world have applauded these efforts, the future of Kenya's fauna remains precarious. With the country's human population expected to double before the end of the century, man-animal competition for land and scarce resources will increase to the detriment of the latter. Indeed, by 2010, species like the black rhinoceros probably will be extinct and all others severely reduced, if for no other reason than to make way for new farms, roads, towns, and cities.

Uganda

Until recently, Uganda had the most dismal and tragic game preservation record in post-independent East Africa. Poaching initially presented the greatest threat to the country's wildlife. On 8 January 1964, a Game Department spokesman reported that 317 wire snares, 41 foot traps, 37 spears, and 23 game nets had been seized in the Ankole region of southwestern Uganda. He also indicated that although local and central government courts had meted out heavy sentences to most of the 162 convicted poachers who had been operating in Ankole and Kigezi, little could be done to stop illegal hunting in the future.[18]

After Idi Amin's military takeover in 1971, Uganda's fauna suffered tremendously as a result of the country's decline into political, economic, and social chaos. Uganda's disintegration precipitated an ecological disaster that—according to Paul Tamukeede, Acting Director of the Uganda National Parks in 1979—cost the lives of about 250,000 wild animals in the country's national parks and game reserves. Most died at the hands of Amin's senior military officers, who poached for skins, ivory, rhinoceros horn, and meat.

To compound the problem, the collapse of the tourist trade meant no foreign currency to pay for vehicles and weapons needed to maintain effective anti-poaching patrols. As a result, illegal killings increased dramatically throughout Uganda's national parks. In Murchison Falls National Park (also known as Kabalega Falls), for example, the

---

17. *The Weekly Review*, 18 August 1995, pp. 17-18. To achieve a more realistic balance between man and animal, a five-member team, commissioned by the Kenya Wildlife Service, recommended several measures, including the establishment of a pension fund to compensate victims of wild animal attacks, a lifting of the big game hunting ban to encourage profitable consumptive use of wildlife, and the enactment of new legislation to boost higher earnings from wildlife.

18. *EAS*, 8 January 1964, p. 3.

elephant population dropped from approximately 15,000 in 1972, to about 2,500 in 1976, to just over 2,000 in 1978. The park's rhinoceros herd fell from fifty in 1971, to ten by the end of 1978. In Queen Elizabeth National Park, which was founded in 1952 by official act, most elephants and other large game animals had disappeared by early 1979. When the Tanzanian People's Defence Force invaded Uganda in the spring of 1979 to help the Uganda National Liberation Army overthrow the Amin regime, much of the country's remaining fauna fell prey to troops hunting for meat. According to Tamukeede, Tanzanian soldiers killed most of Uganda's rhinoceros, buffalo, elephant, and gazelle populations.[19]

Sadly, this carnage continued well into the next decade, largely because subsequent regimes were unable to restore stability. Rebel groups often killed elephants and sold their tusks, using the proceeds to buy arms and ammunition. Many government officials, on the other hand, engaged in the trophy trade for personal profit. Lastly, thousands of displaced persons and refugees relied on wild animals for food.

After seizing power in January 1986, however, Yoweri Museveni promised to end the slaughter of Uganda's wildlife and to rehabilitate the country's tourist industry. Initially the Ugandan government lacked the resources to achieve these goals. As a result, the slaughter of what was left of Uganda's wildlife continued without letup. In early 1986, for example, anti-Museveni soldiers fleeing from Kampala occupied the Paraa Safari Lodge in Murchison Falls National Park and shot any wild animals they could find for food. Such incidents continued into the early 1990s, especially in areas where rebel or government forces were quartered or where poachers or other criminal elements were active. Large numbers of Sudanese People's Liberation Army personnel who had taken refuge in Kidepo Valley National Park also relied on wild animals as a food source.[20]

As it succeeded in restoring stability to much of Uganda and in attracting ever increasing amounts of aid from the international donor community, the Museveni regime began to allocate resources to the wildlife and tourism sectors. In early 1991, for example, Kampala unveiled a $75-million program to rehabilitate hotels and game lodges to lure western tourists back to Uganda.[21] On 29 November 1993, James Wapakabulo, the Minister of Tourism, Wildlife and Antiquities, unveiled a ten-year plan to promote the tourism industry. The $53.8-million rehabilitation of Entebbe International Airport and the abolition of a visa requirement for nationals from 33 European, North American, and

---

19. *The Sunday Telegraph*, 8 July 1979, p. 2.

20. *Africa Analysis*, 13 December 1991, p. 14. The Ugandan government allowed the Sudanese rebels to remain in Kidepo Valley National Park to discourage the Sudanese government from providing aid to anti-Museveni elements which had sought refuge in southern Sudan.

21. *African Economic Digest*, 3 June 1991, p. 23.

Asian countries further stimulated tourism. More importantly, by 1996, the Ugandan government had expanded the number of national parks to ten (Queen Elizabeth, Murchison Falls, Kidepo Valley, Lake Mburo, Kibale, Ruwenzori, Bwindi Impenetrable Forest, Mgahinga Gorilla, Mount Elgon, and Semliki Valley).

By the late 1990s, these and other efforts, coupled with increasingly strict conservation policies, started to pay dividends. Uganda's elephant population increased from about 1,000 at the time of Idi Amin's 1979 down fall to more than 3,000 a decade later.[22] The country's gorilla population, which supposedly numbered about 300 in mid-1995, benefited from a $5-million trust fund for its protection in the Mgahinga-Bwindi Impenetrable Forest National Parks.[23] These successes helped tourism to become one of the most rapidly expanding sectors in the Ugandan economy with an annual growth rate of about 20 per cent.[24] However, unlike Kenya and Tanzania, Uganda hopes to lessen the impact large numbers of visitors have on national parks by stressing eco-tourism rather than mass-tourism.

Despite this dramatic turn around, the well-being of Uganda's fauna is far from secure. According to the United Nations Fund for Population Activities, Uganda's population will increase from approximately 16.5 million in 1991 (the date of the last census) to about 53 million in 2025.[25] Such a spectacular increase will intensify competition for scare government resources and human encroachment on wildlife areas. Minimal economic opportunities will mean that poaching and other illegal activities will pose far greater threats to Uganda's fauna than they do today. These harsh realities will make it extremely difficult to maintain a network of ten national parks. What is more likely is that a modicum of Uganda's fauna will survive in a few well-guarded parks that probably will be fenced off from the rest of the country.

Tanzania

In many respects Tanzania, during the first years of its independence, led East Africa in fauna preservation. According to Bernard Grzimek, the German naturalist noted for his work in the Serengeti, the post-colonial government succeeded in obtaining international

22. *The New Vision*, 31 January 1991, p. 1.

23. *The Indian Ocean Newsletter*, 1 July 1995, p. 7.

24. *The New Vision*, 27 September 1995, p. 15.

25. *The New Vision*, 23 July 1991, p. 8.

26. Quoted in *EAS*, 16 February 1965, p. 4.

aid for development of its national parks.[26] The Tanzanian government also supported the activities of the East African College of Wildlife Management located at Mweka, ten miles from Moshi on the slopes of Mount Kilimanjaro. This school started the Africanization of East Africa's game departments, graduating its first class of eighteen African game wardens and thirty-four African game assistants in 1965.[27]

Although the Africanization program was politically popular, John Owen, Director of Tanzania National Parks, believed that "with the Africanization of European jobs in the early 1970s, the wildlife industry lost much of its international appeal, and the decline of the Tanzanian government interest followed swiftly." For the East African College of Wildlife Management, whose operating budget had been met almost entirely by overseas aid, the result was disastrous. According to Hugh Lamprey, the school's first principal, the College's effectiveness continued to decline until the breakup of the East African Community in 1977.[28]

To make matters worse, a large section of Tanzania's public opinion—inflamed by the government's calls to destroy capitalism and embrace socialism—rejected wildlife preservation as a means to secure economic gain. The so-called "tourism debate" appeared in The Standard for about three months during the middle of 1970. Readers lashed out at what they perceived to be neocolonial exploitation; namely, hordes of foreign tourists demanding and receiving services such as luxury hotels, plumbing, and comprehensive medical facilities that were unavailable to the ordinary Tanzanian.[29]

> As this anti-tourism attitude hardened, funds for game preservation became scare. In 1976, Game Department officials Brian Nicholson and Alan Rodgers submitted a report to the Ministry of Natural Resources and Tourism in which they deplored the withdrawal of financial support from the Selous Game Reserve. The enforced reduction of game wardens, engineers, and mechanics. . .the loss of all but 10 per cent of the reserve's vehicles due to mechanical breakdown, and the virtual cessation of patrolling, with the result that the poaching activities brought under control ten years before were on the increase once again.[30]

When the ministry failed to respond to this charge, Nicholson resigned and left the

---

27. *EAS*, 3 March 1965, p. 6.

28. Quoted in Peter Matthiessen, *Sand Rivers* (New York: The Viking Press, 1981), p. 22.

29. The entire collection of correspondence is contained in I.G. Shivji, *Tourism and Socialist Development* (Dar es Salaam: Tanzania Publishing House, 1973).

30. Matthiessen, *Sand Rivers*, pp. 22-3.

country, claiming that anyone interested in preserving Tanzania's fauna was beating his head against a wall.[31]

In the next few years, staff shortages, government lethargy, and increased poaching laid waste to Tanzania's national parks and game reserves. By 1986, according to the Nairobi-based regional office of the International Union for the Conservation of Nature and Natural Resources (IUCN), the Tanzanian government had failed to stop poaching. To make matters worse, high prices had restricted the number of foreign tourists who visited Tanzania. This denied the national parks much needed revenue and reduced the incentive to protect wildlife.

After becoming president in 1985, Ali Hassan Mwinyi argued for economic liberal-ization and an end to rigid socialist rule. As part of this policy, he started to rehabilitate Tanzania's tourist industry and to emphasize the need to preserve the country's wildlife. To attract more foreign tourists, the state-owned Tanzania Tourist Corporation (TTC) embarked on a program to refurbish the nation's hotels. Tanzania also encouraged foreign and private investors to operate safari lodges and camps.

Wildlife officials supported Mwinyi's strategy by launching the largest anti-poaching operation in Tanzania's history. Costing about $14,000 a day, Operation Uhai, which began in mid-1989, involved deploying military and security personnel to the country's national parks and arresting approximately 1,500 poachers. The Tanzanian government hoped that Operation Uhai would stabilize its elephant herds, which had declined from 184,872 in 1977 to 87,088 in 1989. By mid-1995, it had become evident that Operation Uhai had exceeded initial expectations. According to the German Association for Technical Cooperation, which worked on several wildlife projects in Tanzania, the elephant population in the Selous Game Reserve had increased from about 30,000 to approximately 52,000 during the 1989-1995 period. On 3 February 1995, the Safari International Club of the United States recognized Tanzania's accomplishments by presenting an award to President Mwinyi for the country's exceptional wildlife conservation record. Interestingly, Tanzania was the first African country to receive this award.

After he became President in late 1995, Benjamin Mkapa took further steps to enhance Tanzania's commitment to fauna preservation. He appointed Bakari Mbano to replace Muhidin Ndolanga as Director of Wildlife, the latter of whom had a reputation for being extremely corrupt.[32] Additionally, Mkapa pledged to implement policies that would en-able local communities to earn more money from tourism.

---

31. *Ibid.*, p. 23.

32. *New African*, June 1995, p. 33.

In contrast to these achievements, Tanzania, like Kenya and Uganda, must establish a politically acceptable balance between the need for strict wildlife conservation policies and escalating demands for land by a growing human population. In many areas, local communities have long-standing hostilities toward what they perceive as the Tanzanian government's preferential treatment of wild animals.

For example, the Maasai people who live around the Ngorongoro Conservation Area in north central Tanzania repeatedly have complained that officials adopt conservation policies without consulting with them. The latest incident occurred in late 1995, when the Ngorongoro Pastoralist Survival Trust, which protects the rights of the Maasai, accused a consultant who worked for the IUCN of writing a proposal for managing the Ngorongoro Conservation Area without getting the approval of the local Maasai authorities. Such episodes are a reflection of a common problem throughout East Africa; namely that many Africans believe that they get little or nothing from fauna preservation. Resolving this dilemma will require a fundamental redistribution of tourist revenues to the local level.

Conclusion

The history of game preservation in East Africa is a tragic story. For almost seventy years, British colonial authorities sought to resolve the man-animal conflict by trying to devise a policy that would preserve fauna without impeding East Africa's economic development. Accomplishing such a difficult task would have been taxing under the best of circumstances. In colonial East Africa, it was especially arduous as conservation efforts rarely received adequate resources or sufficient political support. In contrast, those who advocated widespread social and economic development often possessed substantial assets and considerable political influence. Thus, many man-animal conflicts were resolved in favor of the former.

Nevertheless, there were several important preservation successes during the colonial period, the most significant of which were the establishment of a network of game reserves and an embryonic national park system. Growing international concern about the fate of East Africa's wildlife also became a positive force in the struggle to preserve the region's wild animals. However, although these triumphs facilitated the preservation of East Africa's wildlife heritage, untold millions of wild animals died as a result of various pressures caused by a rapidly growing human population, harmful land use practices, and widespread social and economic development.

For East Africa's post-independence governments, the lessons of the colonial era should have served as guidelines for formulating ecologically sound land use and wildlife preservation policies, which took into account the needs of a growing human population. Instead, conservation programs often proceeded in a haphazard manner as inadequately staffed and financed wildlife agencies struggled against a staggering array of problems, including poaching, illegal trafficking in ivory and other animal trophies, environmentally harmful social and economic development policies, and official corruption. Moreover, as the region's human population increased, and more land was cultivated or sacrificed for roads, towns, tourist facilities, schools, hospitals, and airports, destruction of fauna continued apace. In view of the fact that this process was inevitable and could not have been stopped or reversed, it is astonishing that so much wildlife survived the colonial period. For this, the world owes a debt of gratitude to the few men who devoted their professional lives to East Africa's wild animals.

In recent years, Kenya, Uganda, and Tanzania, all of which have benefited from tourist revenues, have taken dramatic steps to arrest the destruction of East Africa's wildlife. All three countries have supported the Convention on International Trade in Endangered Species of Wild Fauna and Flora (CITES) ban on ivory trading.[33] Additionally, Nairobi, Dar-es-Salaam, and Kampala have devoted considerable resources to anti-poaching and conservation programs. The number of national parks or otherwise protected areas also have increased in each of these nations.

Despite this progress, East Africa's fauna faces a highly uncertain future. Apart from continued human population growth, spreading urbanization; growing demands for agricultural land; pollution, especially in the national parks of game reserves; and illegal poaching are ever present threats to wildlife preservation efforts. As a result of these problems, some conservationists are convinced that the only way to preserve the region's wild animals is to fence-in some or all of East Africa national parks and game reserves. Critics oppose such a step because it would interdict animal migration routes and would transform East Africa's national parks into zoos. Even if Kenya, Uganda, and Tanzania fenced-in their national parks, the needs of modern society would continue to place tremendous pressure on these fragile eco-systems. The lucrative tourism trade, historically seen as one of the best arguments for wildlife preservation, also has become a threat to East Africa's fauna. By the mid-1990s, East Africa annually received nearly a million foreign tourists, the majority of which visited national parks or game reserves. Heavy vehicular traffic, the construction of luxury hotels and other amenities, and the concomitant growth

---

33. For a discussion of CITES and its efforts to stop ivory poaching, see David Harland, "Jumping on the 'Ban' Wagon: Efforts to Save the African Elephant," *The Fletcher Forum of World Affairs* 14/2 (Summer, 1990), pp. 284-300. Also, see United Nations Environment Programme (UNEP), *The African Elephant* (Nairobi: UNEP, 1989); Ian Parker, *Ivory Crisis* (London: Chatto and Windus, 1983); and Ivory Trade Review Group (ITRG), *The Ivory Trade and the Future of the African Elephant* Vol. I (Oxford: International Development Center, 1989).

George Adamson. Until his untimely death in 1989, George Adamson was the acknowledged "lion man" of Africa.
Courtesy of Gerald Rilling

The author on safari in the Serengeti.

Courtesy of the author

of the number of African and non-African workers and support staffs all have a significant negative impact on the well-being of these parks and reserves.

In summary, independent East Africa has been no more successful than colonial East Africa in resolving the man-animal conflict. As the region continues to grow and prosper, it will become increasingly difficult for wild animals to live with their human neighbors. To be sure, the region's governments will continue to make impressive short-term gains enabling large numbers of some species to survive into the next century. However, in the long term, the growing needs of a rapidly expanding human population will cause a drastic reduction in East Africa's fauna, which increasingly be confined to areas tightly controlled by humans. In such an atmosphere, East Africa's fauna will be little more than curiosities. When this happens the world will, indeed, have lost a paradise.

Selected Bibliography

1. Unpublished Documents
   (A). In the United Kingdom
   (B). In the United States
2. Oral Sources
3. Manuscript Collections
4. Government Publications
   (A). Great Britain
   (B). East Africa Protectorate/Kenya
   (C). Tanganyika Territory
   (D). Uganda Protectorate/Uganda
   (E). Zanzibar
   (F). East Africa High Commission
5. Books
6. Articles
7. Newspapers and Journals
8. Dissertations

Uupublished Documents

(A). In the United Kingdom
   (i) Public Record Office, London.
      Foreign Office Records
      Series F.O. 2 Africa. General Correspondence.
      Series F.O. 403 Africa. Confidential Prints.
      Colonial Office Records
      Series C.O. 323 Colonies. General. Original Correspondence.
      Series C.O. 457 East Africa and Uganda Protectorates. Official Gazette, 1899-1907.
      Series C.O. 519 East Africa and Uganda Protectorates. OriginalCorrespondence.
      Series C.O. 533 East Africa Protectorate/Kenya.
      Original Correspondence.
      Series C.O. 536 Uganda Protectorate. Original from 1905.
      Series C.O. 544 East Africa Protectorate/Kenya. Sessional Papers.
      Series C.O. 685 Uganda Protectorate. Sessional Papers.
      Series C.O. 691 Tanganyika Territory. Original Correspondence. Series C.O. 736 Tanganyika Territory. Sessional Papers.
      Series C.O. 822 East Africa. Original Correspondence.

Series C.O. 885 Colonial Office Confidential Prints.

Series C.O. 879 Africa. Confidential Prints. Colonial Office List, 1900-63.

Cabinet Papers

CAB 58 Tse-Tse Fly Committee

(ii) Institute of Commonwealth Studies, London. Foreign Office Confidential Prints 1886-1905.

(B). In the United States

(i) Kenya National Archives, Syracuse University.

Provincial and District Annual and Quarterly Reports.

Political Record Books

Handing Over Reports

Miscellaneous Reports

Intelligence Reports

(ii) Tanganyika National Archives, Michigan State University.

Provincial and District Record Books.

Oral Sources

(A). Interviews

Sir Francis Loyd 11 May 1979 (London)

Noel Simon 14 May 1979 (London)

John Burton 21 May 1979 (London)

Ian Grimwood 11 June 1979 (Nairobi)

Hugh Lamprey 14 June 1979 (Nairobi)

Rennie Bere 28-29 July 1979 (Bude,UK)

John Owen 5 August 1979 (Tunbridge Wells,UK)

John Webster 9 August 1979 (London)

Manuscript Collections

(A). In the United Kingdom

(i) Museum of Natural History Library, London.

Charles Pitman Papers

(ii) School of Oriental and African Studies, University of London.

Sir William Mackinnon Papers

(iii) Rhodes House, Oxford.

Private Papers:

John Ainsworth

Mervyn Cowie

Francis Hall

C.W. Hobley

J.H. Patterson

Sir Patrick Renison

Miscellaneous Papers:

Collection of Materials Pertaining to the Serengeti National Park

(iv) Bere Papers, in Rennie Bere's possession.

Huxley Papers, in author's possession.

Government Publications

(A). Great Britain

Papers Relating to the Mombasa Railway Survey and Uganda, C. 6555 (1892).

Report by Sir A. Hardinge on the Condition and Progress of the East Africa Protectorate From Its Establishment to the 20th July 1897, C. 8683 (1897).

Report of Sir A. Hardinge on the British East Africa Protectorate for the Year 1897-98, C. 9125 (1899).

Report by H.M. Commissioner on the East Africa Protectorate, Cd. 769 (1901).

Report by H.M. Commissioner on the East Africa Protectorate, Cd. 1626 (1903).

Report on the East Africa Protectorate for the Year 1903-04, Cd. 2331 (1904).

Reports Relating to the Administration of the East Africa Protectorate, Cd. 2740 (1905).

Annual Reports, East Africa Protectorate, 1905-1919.

Annual Reports, Colony and Protectorate of Kenya, 1920-1963.

Annual Reports, Uganda Protectorate, 1905-1963.

Correspondence Relating to the Preservation of Wild Animals in Africa, Cd. 3189 (1906).

Further Correspondence Relating to the Preservation of Wild Animals in Africa, Cd. 4472 (1909); Cd. 5136 (1910); Cd. 5775 (1911); and Cd. 6671 (1913).

Annual Reports, Tanganyika Territory, published in the Colonial series beginning in 1924.

Agreements Concluded at the International Conference for the Protection of the Fauna and Flora of Africa, Cmd. 4453 (1933).

Statement of Policy on Colonial Development and Welfare, Cmd. 6175 (1940).

The British Territories in East and Central Africa 1945-1950, Cmd. 7987 (1950).

Report of the East Africa Royal Commission, 1953-55, Cmd. 9475 (1955).

(B). East Africa Protectorate/Kenya

Blue Books, East Africa Protectorate, 1905-1919.

Blue Books, Colony and Protectorate of Kenya, 1920-1950.

Department *Annual Reports*:

Game Department, 1910-1963, not published during the First World War.

Department of Agriculture, 1908-1963.

Department of Forestry, 1910-1963.

Veterinary Department, 1921-1963.

Legislative Council, *Minutes and Debates*, 1907-1963.

Official Gazette, East Africa Protectorate, 1903-1919.

Official Gazette, Colony and Protectorate of Kenya, 1920-1963.

Royal National Parks of Kenya, *Report*, 1946-1964.

Interim Report of the Game Policy Committee, (1943).

Second Interim Report of the Game Policy Committee, (1945).

Report of the 1956 Game Policy Committee, (1958).

(C). Tanganyika Territory

Blue Books, Tanganyika Territory, 1921-1950.

Department *Annual Reports*:

Game Department, 1921-1963.

Department of Agriculture, 1923-1963.

Forestry Department, 1920-1963.

Medical Department, 1920-1963.

Veterinary Department, 1921-1963.

Legislative Council, *Proceedings and Sessional Papers*, 1926-1963.

Official Gazette, Tanganyika Territory, 1919-1950.

Reports, Provincial Commissioners, 1929-1950.

Tanganyika National Parks, *Report and Accounts of the Board of Trustees*, 1951-1962.

Dispatches to and from the Secretary of State Regarding the Indiscriminate Slaughter of Big Game on the Serengeti Plains, (1929).

The Serengeti National Park, (1956).

Report of the Serengeti Committee of Enquiry, (1957).

Proposals for Reconstituting the Serengeti National Park, (1958).

The CCTA/IUCN Symposium on the Conservation of Nature and Natural Resources in Modern African States, (1961).

(D). Uganda Protectorate

Blue Books, Uganda Protectorate, 1907-1963.

Department *Annual Reports*:

Department of Agriculture, 1913-1963.

Forest Department, 1918-1963.

Game Department, 1925-1963.

Department of Veterinary Services and Animal Industry, 1921-1963.

Legislative Council, *Proceedings*, 1939-1962.

Official Gazette, Uganda Protectorate, 1903-1950.

Uganda National Parks, *Report and Accounts of the Trustees of the Uganda National Parks*, 1955-1963.

Report on the Control of Elephants in Uganda, (1923).

Game Preservation and Economic Development, (1928).

The Game Department Handbook, (1937).

A Development Plan for Uganda, (1947).

Report of the Uganda National Parks Committee, (1950).

Memorandum by Government on Proposed Alterations to the Queen Elizabeth Park Boundary, (1958).

Select Committee of the Legislative Council Appointed on 13 March, 1959 to Consider the Game (Preservation and Control) Bill, (1959).

(E). Zanzibar

The Zanzibar Gazette, 1894-1900.

(F). East Africa High Commission

Fauna of British Eastern and Central Africa, (1948).

Fauna of British Eastern and Central Africa, (1952).

Fauna of British Eastern and Central Africa, (1956).

Books

Adamson, George. *A Lifetime With Lions*. New York: Doubleday and Company, Inc., 1968.

American Committee for International Wild Life Protection. *African Game Protection*. Cambridge, Mass.: American Committee for International Wild Life Protection, 1933.

Anderson, G.H. *African Safaris*. Nakuru: Nakuru Press, n.d.

Archer, Sir G. *Personal and Historical Memoirs of an East African Administrator*. London: Oliver and Boyd, 1963.

Beard, Peter H. *The End of the Game*. New York: Doubleday and Company, Inc., 1977.

Bell, W.D.M. *Karamoja Safari*. London: Gollancz, 1949.

Bell, W.D.M. *The Wanderings of an Elephant Hunter*. London: Country Life, 1923.

Bell, Hesketh H. *Glimpses of a Governor's Life*. London: Sampson Low, Marston and Company, Ltd., 1946.

Bere, R.M. *The Wild Mammals of Uganda and Neighboring Regions of East Africa*. London: Longmans, 1962.

Bille, G. Ahefeldt. *Tandalla*. London: Routledge and Kegan Paul, 1951.

Bland-Sutton, J. *Men and Creatures in Uganda*. London: Hutchinson and Company, 1933.

Blixen-Finecke, Bror von. *African Hunter*. London: Alfred A. Knopf, 1938.

Blunt, David E. *Elephant*. Boston and New York: Houghton Mifflin Company, 1933.

Bolton, Kenneth (ed.). *The Lion and the Lily: A Guide to Kenya*. London: Geoffrey Bles, 1962.

Bridges, Thomas C. *Wardens of the Wild*. London: George G. Harrap and Company, Ltd., 1937.

Brodhurst-Hill, Eve. *The Youngest Lion: Early Farming Days in Kenya*. London: Hutchinson and Company, 1934.

Bromhead, Walter S. *What's What in Kenya Highlands*. Nairobi: The East African Standard Ltd., 1923.

Bull, Bartle. *Safari: A Chronicle of Adventure*. New York: Viking, 1988.

Bulpin, Thomas V. *The Hunter is Death*. Cape Town: Books of Africa, 1968.

Burton, Richard F. *The Lake Regions of Central Africa*. 2 vols. London: Longman, Green, Longman and Roberts, 1860.

Caldwell, Keith. *Report on a Faunal Survey in Eastern and Central Africa*. London: Society for the Preservation of the Fauna of the Empire, (Occasional Paper #8), 1948.

Carnegie, V.M. *A Kenyan Farm Diary*. London: William Blackwood & Sons, 1931.

Chapman, Abel. *On Safari: Big Game Hunting in British East Africa*. London: Edward Arnold, 1908.

Clyde, D.F. *History of the Medical Services of Tanganyika*. Dar es Salaam: Government Press, 1962.

Cloudsley-Thompson, J.L. *Animal Twilight: Man and Game in Eastern Africa*. London: Dufour, 1967.

Cone, L. Winston and J.F. Lipscomb. *The History of Kenya Agriculture*. Nairobi: University Press of Africa, 1972.

Copley, Hugh and R.F. Mayer. *The East African Sportsmans Handbook*. Nairobi: The East African Standard Ltd., 1934.

Coupland, Sir Reginald. *The Exploitation of East Africa*. London: Faber and Faber, 1939.

Cowie, Mervyn. *I Walk with Lions*. New York: The Macmillan Company, 1964.

Cranworth, Lord. *A Colony in the Making*. London: Macmillan and Company, Ltd., 1912.

Cranworth, Lord. *Kenya Chronicles*. London: Macmillan and Company, Ltd., 1939.

Cullen, Anthony and Sidney Downey. *Saving the Game*. London: Jarrolds, 1960.

Cumming, R.G. *Five Years of a Hunter's Life in the Far Interior of South Africa*. 2 vols. London: John Murray, 1850.

Dilke, C.W. *Problems of Greater Britain*. 2 vols. London: Macmillan and Company, 1890.

Douglas-Hamilton, Iain and Oria. *Among the Elephants*. London: Collins and Harvill, 1976.

Eliot, Sir Charles. *The East Africa Protectorate*. New York: Barnes and Noble, 1966.

Fitter, R. and P. Scott. *The Penitent Butchers*. London: Fauna P-reservation Society, 1978.

Foran, W. Robert. *A Breath of the Wilds*. London: Robert Hale Ltd., 1958.

Foran, W. Robert. *A Hunter's Saga*. London: Robert Hale, 1961.

Foran, W. Robert. *Kill or be Killed: The Rambling Reminiscences of an Amateur Hunter*. New York: St. Martin's Press, 1988.

Ford, J. *The Role of Trypanosomiases in African Ecology*. Oxford: The Clarendon Press, 1971.

Galbraith, J.S. *Mackinnon and East Africa 1878-1895: A Study in the 'New Imperialism.'* Cambridge: Cambridge University Press, 1972.

Gann, L.H. and Peter Duignan. *White Settlers in Tropical Africa*. Westport: Greenwood Press, 1977.

Gillman, C. *A Population Map of Tanganyika Territory*. Dar es Salaam: Government Printer, 1936.

Graham, Alistair. *The Gardeners of Eden*. London: George Allen and Unwin Ltd., 1973.

Grant, James A. *A Walk Across Africa*. London: William Blackwood and Sons Ltd., 1864.

Grzimek, Bernhard and Michael. *Serengeti Shall Not Die*. London: Collins, 1965.

Harris, N.D. *Europe and Africa*. New York: Negro Universities Press, 1969.

Hayden, Sherman Strong. *The International Protection of Wild Life*. New York: Columbia University Press, 1942.

Herne, Brian. *Uganda Safaris*. Tulsa, OK: Winchester Press, 1979.

Hill, J.F.R. and J.P. Moffett (eds.). *Tanganyika: A Review of Its Resources and Their Development*. Dar es Salaam: Government Printer, 1955.

Hill, M.F. *Permanent Way*. 2 vols. Nairobi: East African Railways and Harbours, 1961, c. 1958.

Holman, Dennis. *The Elephant People*. London: John Murray, 1967.

Holman, Dennis. *Elephants at Sun Down: The Story of Bill Woodley*. London: W.H. Allen, 1978.

Holman, Dennis. *Inside Safari Hunting*. New York: G.P. Putnam's Sons, 1969.

Horrobin, D.F. *A Guide to Kenya and Northern Tanzania*. New York: Charles Scribner's Sons, 1971.

Hunter, John A. *Hunter*. New York: Harper, 1952.

Hunter, John A. *Hunter's Tracks*. New York: Appleton-Century-Crofts, Inc., 1957.

Hunter, John A. *White Hunter: The Adventures of a Big Game Hunter in Africa*. London: Seeley, Service and Company, Ltd., 1938.

Huxley, Elspeth and Hugo van Lawick. *Last Days in Eden*. New York: The Amaryllis Press, 1984.

Huxley, Elspeth. *White Man's Country: Lord Delamere and the Making of Kenya*. 2 vols. London: Chatto and Windus, 1974.

Huxley, Julian. *The Conservation of Wild Life and Natural Habitats in Central and East Africa*. Paris: UNESCO, 1961.

Huxley, Juliette. *Wild Lives of Africa*. New York: Harper and Row, 1963.

Iliffe, John. *A Modern History of Tanganyika*. Cambridge: Cambridge University Press, 1979.s

Ionides, C.J.P. *Mambas and Man-Eaters, A Hunter's Story*. New York: Holt, Rinehart and Winston, 1965.

Ise, J. *Our National Park Policy: A Critical History*. Baltimore: Johns Hopkins Press, 1961.

Ivory Trade Review Group, *The Ivory Trade and the Future of the African Elephant*. Vol I Oxford: International Development Center, 1989.

Jackson, Sir Frederick J. *Early Days in East Africa*. London: Edward Arnold and Company, 1930.

Jahnke, Hans E. *Conservation and Utilization of Wildlife in Uganda*. Munchen: Ifo-Institut fur Wirtschaftsforschung, 1974.

Johnson, V.E. *Pioneering for Christ in East Africa*. Rock Island, IL: Augustana Book Concern, 1948.

Johnston, A. *The Life and Letters of Sir Harry Johnston*. New York: Cape and Smith, 1929.

Johnston, Sir Harry H. *The Story of My Life*. Indianapolis: Bobbs Merrill, 1923.

..................*The Uganda Protectorate*. 2 vols. New York: Dodd, Mead and Company, 1902.

Karugire, S.R. *A Political History of Uganda*. Nairobi: Heinemann, 1980.

Keller, W. Phillip. *Africa's Wild Glory*. London: Jarrolds, 1959.

Kinloch, Bruce. *The Shambaa Raiders: Memories of a Game Warden*. London: Collins and Harvill Press, 1972.

Kittenberger, K. *Big Game Hunting and Collecting in East Africa, 1903-1926*. London: Edward Arnold and Company, 1929.

Kjekshus, Helge. *Ecology Control and Economic Development in East African History*. London: Heinemann, 1977.

Koenig, Oskar. *Pori Tupu*. New York: McGraw Hill Book Company, Inc., 1954.

Kuczynski, R.R. *Demographic Survey of the British Colonial Empire*. Vol. II London: Oxford University Press, 1949.

Laws, R.M., Parker, I.S.C., and R.C.B. Johnstone. *Elephants and Their Habitats: The Ecology of Elephants in North Bunyoro, Uganda*. Oxford: Clarendon Press, 1975.

Leakey, L.S.B. *Adam's Ancestors*. London: Methuen and Company, 1953.

Livingstone, D. and C. *Narrative of An Expedition to the Zambezi and Its T-ributaries*. London: John Murray, 1865.

Livingstone, David. *Missionary Travels and Researches in South Africa*. London: John Murray, 1857.

Loveridge, Arthur. *Many Happy Days I've Squandered*. New York: Harper and Brothers Publishers, 1944.

Low, D.A. and Alison Smith. *History of East Africa*. Vol. III Oxford: Clarendon Press, 1976.

Luck, Anne. *Charles Stokes in Africa*. Nairobi: East Africa Publishing House, n.d.

Lyell, Denis D. *African Adventures: Letters From Famous Big Game Hunters*. New York: E.P. Dutton, 1935.

McCutcheon, John T. *In Africa*. Indianapolis: Bobbs Merrill, 1980.

McDermott, P.L. *British East Africa or I.B.E.A.*. London: Chapman and Hall, 1895.

MacDonald, Malcolm. *Treasure of Kenya*. London: Collins, 1965.

McKelvey, J.J. *Man Against Tsetse*. Ithaca: Cornell University Press, 1973.

Marsh, Zoe and G.W. Kingsnorth. *An Introduction to the History of East Africa*. Cambridge: Cambridge University Press, 1965.

Matthiessen, Peter. *Sand Rivers*. New York: The Viking Press, 1981.

Matthiessen, Peter and E. Porter. *The Tree Where Man Was Born*. New York: Cresent, 1975.

Maydon, H.C. *Big Game Shooting in Africa*. London: Seeley, Service and Company, Ltd. 1932.

Meinertzhagen, Richard. *Kenya Diary 1902-1906*. Edinburgh: Oliver and Boyd, 1957.

Mitchell, Sir Philip. *African Afterthoughts*. London: Hutchinson and Company, 1954.

Moore, Audrey. *Serengeti*. New York: Charles Scribner's Sons, 1939.

Morgan, W.T.W. *East Africa: Its People and Resources*. Nairobi: Oxford University Press, 1966.

Moss, Cynthia. *Elephant Memories*. New York: William Morrow and Company, Inc., 1988.

Mungeam, G.H. *British Rule in Kenya, 1895-1912*. London: Oxford University Press, 1966.

Nash, T.A.M. *Africa's Bane: The Tsetse Fly*. London: Collins, 1969.

New, Charles. *Life, Wanderings and Labours in Eastern Africa*. London: Hodder and Stoughton, 1873.

Oliver, Roland (ed.). *The Cambridge History of Africa*. Vol. III Cambridge: Cambridge University Press, 1977.

..............................*Harry Johnston and the Scramble for Africa*. New York: St. Martin's Press, 1957.

..............................and G. Mathew. *History of East Africa*. Vol. I Oxford: The Clarendon Press, 1968.

Ouma, Joseph. *Evolution of Tourism in East Africa (1900-2000)*. Nairobi: East African Literature Bureau, 1970.

Parker, Ian. *Ivory Crisis*. London: Chatto and Windus, 1983.

Patterson, John H. I*n the Grip of the Nyika*. London: Macmillan and Company Ltd., 1910.

Patterson, John H. *The Man-Eaters of Tsavo*. London: MacMillan and Company Ltd., 1907.

Pearsall, W.H. *Report on an Ecological Survey of the Serengeti National Park*. London: Fauna Preservation Society, 1957.

Percival, A.B. *A Game Ranger on Safari*. London: Nisbet, 1928.

Percival, A.B. *A Game Ranger's Note Book*. New York: George H. Doran Company, 1924.

Pitman, C.R.S. *A Game Warden Among His Charges*. London: Nisbet, 1931.

....................................*A Game Warden Takes Stock*. London: Nisbet, 1942.

Poole, A.L. *From Domesday Book to Magna Carta 1087-1216*. Oxford: The Clarendon Press, 1951.

Powicke, M. *The Thirteenth Century 1216-1307*. Oxford: The Clarendon Press, 1953.

Robins, Eric. *Africa's Wild Life: Survival or Extinction*. London: Odhams Press Ltd., 1963.

Roosevelt, Theodore. *African Game Trials*. New York: Charles Scribner's Sons, 1910.

Rushby, George G. *No More the Tusker*. London: W.H. Allen, 1965.

Russell, E. Walter. *A Management Policy for the Tanzania National Parks*. London: Fauna Preservation Society, 1968.

Sandford, G.R. *An Administrative and Political History of the Masai Reserve*. London: Waterlow and Sons, Ltd., 1919.

Sayers, G.F. (ed.). *Handbook of Tanganyika*. London: Macmillan and Company, 1930.

Schweinfurth, Georg. *The Heart of Africa*. 2 vols. London: Sampson Low, Marston, Low, and Searle, 1874.

Seaton, Harry. *Lion in the Morning*. London: John Murray, 1963.

Sheldrick, Daphne. *Animal Kingdom: The Story of Tsavo, The Great African Game Park*. Indianapolis: The Bobbs Merrill Company, Inc., 1973.

Shorter, A. *Chiefship in Western Tanzania: A Political History of Kimbu*. Oxford: The Clarendon Press, 1972.

Siedentopf, A.R. *The Last Stronghold of Big Game*. London: Hodder and Stoughton Ltd., 1947.

Shiveji, I.G. (ed.). *Tourism and Socialist Development*. Dar es Salaam: Tanzania Publishing House, 1973.

Simon, Noel. *Between the Sunlight and the Thunder: The Wildlife of Kenya*. Boston: Houghton Mifflin Company, 1963.

Speke, John Hanning. *What Led to the Discovery of the Source of the Nile*. London: William Blackwood and Sons, Ltd., 1864.

Stigand, C.H. *The Game of British East Africa*. London: Horace Cox, 1909.

Swynnerton, C.F.M. *The Tsetse Flies of East Africa*. London: Royal Entomological Society, 1937.

Tanganyika and Kenya Wild Life Societies. *Comments on the Tanganyika Government's White Paper Entitled "The Serengeti Park"*. Nairobi: D.A. Hawkins, Ltd., 1956.

Thomas, H.B. and R. Scott. *Uganda*. London: Oxford University Press, 1935.

Thomas, T.S. *Jubaland and the Northern Frontier District*. Nairobi: Uganda Railway Press, 1917.

Thomson, Joseph. *Through Masai Land*. London: Sampson, Low, Marston, Searle and Riverton, 1885.

Tignor, Robert C. *The Colonial Transformation of Kenya: The Kamba, Kikuyu, and Maasai from 1900 to 1939*. Princeton: Princeton University Press, 1976.

Trzebinski, Errol. *The Kenya Pioneers*. London: Heinemann, 1985.

United Nations Environment Programme. *The African Elephant*. Nairobi: UNEP, 1989.

Van Zwanenberg, R.M.A. with Anne King. *An Economic History of Kenya and Uganda 1800-1970*. London: Macmillan Press, Ltd., 1977.

Western David. I*n the Dust of Kilimanjaro*. Washington, D.C.: Island Press/Shearwater Books, 1997.

Willock, Colin. *The Enormous Zoo: A Profile of the Uganda National Parks*. New York: Harcourt, Brace and World Inc., 1964.

Willoughby, Captain Sir John C. *East Africa and its Big Game*. London: Longmans, Green, and Company, 1889.

Wollaston, A.F.R. *From Ruwenzori to the Congo*. London: John Murray, 1908.

Wood, A. *The Groundnut Affair*. London: The Bodley Head, 1950.

Woodward, E.M. *Precis of Information Concerning the Uganda Protectorate*. London: HMSO, 1902.

Yates, C.A. *The Kruger National Park*. London: George Allen and Unwin Ltd., 1935.

Articles

Apted, F.I.C. "Sleeping Sickness in Tanganyika, Past, Present, and Future." *Transactions of the Royal Society of Tropical Medicine and Hygiene*. Vol. LVI (1962), pp. 15-29.

Caldwell, Keith. "The Commercialisation of Game." *Journal of the Society for the Preservation of the Fauna of the Empire*. New Series, Part VII (1927), pp. 83-90.

--------------. "Report of a Further Faunal Survey in East Africa." *Journal of the Society for the Preservation of the Fauna of the Empire*. New Series, Part LXI (March, 1950), pp. 15-22.

"Colonial Development and Welfare." *Journal of the Society for the Preservation of the Fauna of the Empire*. New Series, Part XXXIX (April, 1940), pp. 17-19.

Cowie, Mervyn. "The Royal National Parks," in *The Lion and the Lily: A Guide to Kenya*. ed. Kenneth Bolton. (London: Geoffrey Bles, 1962), pp. 158-171.

Davey, J.B. "The Outbreak of Human Trypanosomiasis (Trypanosoma Rhodesiense Infection) in Mwanza District, Tanganyika Territory." *Transactions of the Royal Society of Tropical Medicine and Hygiene*. Vol. XVII (1924), pp. 474-481.

"Extract From Report on Tanganyika Territory." *Journal of the Society for the Preservation of the Fauna of the Empire*. New Series, Part II (July, 1922), pp. 46-51.

Fairbairn, H. "Sleeping Sickness in Tanganyika Territory, 1922-1946." *Tropical Disease Bulletin*. Vol. 45 (1948), pp. 1-17.

Foran, W. Robert. "National Parks and Game Reserves in East Africa." *African World Annual*. (1950), pp. 45-49.

Haclears, H. "The Albert National Park." *Geographical Magazine*. Vol. IV, No. 4 (February, 1937), pp. 269-286.

Harland, David. "Jumping on the 'Ban' Wagon: Efforts to Save the African Elephant." *The Fletcher Forum of World Affairs*. Vol. 14, No. 2 (Summer, 1990), pp. 284-300.

Hingston, R.W.G. "Plea for National Parks." *Illustrated London News*. (13 December 1930), pp. 1060-1062.

---------------. "Proposed British National Parks for Africa." *Geographical Journal*. Vol. 77, No. 5 (May, 1931), pp. 401-428.

Hobley, C.W. "The London Convention of 1900." *Journal of the Society for the Preservation of the Fauna of the Empire*. New Series, Part XV (August, 1933), pp. 33-49.

"International Congress for the Protection of Nature." *Journal of the Society for the Preservation of the Fauna of the Empire*. New Series, Part XV (December, 1931), pp. 43-52.

"Joint Deputation to H.M. Secretary of State for the Colonies." *Journal of the Society for the Preservation of the Fauna of the Empire*. New Series, Part XI (1930), pp. 11-16.

Kirk, Sir John. "On the 'Tsetse' Fly of Tropical Africa." *Journal of the Linnean Society*. Vol. VIII (1865), pp. 15-56.

Lindsay, W.K. "Elephant Problems and Human Attitudes." *Swara*. Vol. 9, No. 3 (1986), pp. 24-27.

------------------ "Elephants, Trees, and People." *Wildlife News*. Vol. 18, No. 2 (1983), pp. 8-11.

Lonsdale, John and Bruce Berman. "Coping With the Contradictions: The Development of the Colonial State in Kenya, 1895-1914." *Journal of African History*. Vol. 20, No. 4 (1979), pp. 487-505.

Maclean, G. "Sleeping Sickness Measures in Tanganyika Territory." *Kenya and East Africa Medical Journal*. (1930), pp. 120-126.

"Masai Parks." *Wild Life*. (March, 1960), pp. 30-32.

"Masai Tribe Takes Over Amboseli Game Reserve." *Wild Life*. (September/December, 1961), pp. 48-52.

"Minutes of Proceedings at a Deputation From the Society for the Preservation of the Wild Fauna of the Empire Received by the Right Hon. The Earl of Crewe, K.G." *Journal of the Society for the Preservation of the Wild Fauna of the Empire*. Vol. V (1909), pp. 11-27.

"Minutes of Proceedings at a Deputation From the Society for the Preservation of the Fauna of the Empire to the Right Hon. Alfred Lyttelton (His Majesty's Secretary for the Colonies)." *Journal of the Society for the Preservation of the Wild Fauna of the Empire*. Vol. I (1905), pp. 9-18.

"Minutes of Proceedings at a Deputation From the Society for the Preservation of the Wild Fauna of the Empire to the Right Hon. The Earl of Elgin, His Majesty's Secretary of State for the Colonies." *Journal of the Society for the Preservation of the Wild Fauna of the Empire*. Vol. II (1906), pp. 20-32.

Moffett, J.P. "A Strategic Retreat From Tsetse Fly; Uyowa and Bugoma Concentrations 1937." *Tanganyika Notes and Records*. No. 7 (June, 1939), pp. 35-38.

Patterson, John H. "A Report From British East Africa." *Journal of the Society for the Preservation of the Wild Fauna of the Empire*. Vol. III (1907), pp. 73-74.

Pitman, C.R.S. "Uganda's National Parks." *Oryx*. Vol. I, No. 6 (1952), pp. 316-320.

Potts, W.H. and C.H.N. Jackson. "The Shinyanga Game Destruction Experiment." *Bulletin of Entomological Research*. Vol. XLIII (July, 1952), pp. 365-374.

Roberts, A.D. "The Sub-Imperialism of the Baganda." *Journal of African History*. Vol. III, No. 3 (1962), pp. 437-450.

Rushby, George G. "The African Elephant and Its Hunters." *Tanganyika Notes and Records*. No. 17 (June, 1944), pp. 59-63.

Scott, C. "Game and Settlement in Kenya." *United Empire*. Vol. XXVIII, No. 2 (February, 1937), pp. 72-74.

Sharpe, A. "Slaughter by Natives." *Journal of the Society for the Preservation of the Wild Fauna of the Empire*. Vol. I (1905), p. 19.

Simpson, Jack. "The Great Kenya Wildlife Ripoff." *Field and Stream*. Vol. 82, No. 8 (December, 1977), pp. 48, 85-86, 88, 90.

Steinhart, Edward. "Hunters, Paochers and Gamekeepers: Towards a Social History of Hunting in Colonial Kenya." *Journal of African History*. Vol. 30, No. 2 (1989), pp. 247-264.

Stevenson-Hamilton, J. "The Relations Between Game and Tsetse Flies." *Journal of the Society for the Preservation of the Wild Fauna of the Empire*. Vol. VI (1913), pp. 88-89.

Swynnerton, C.F.M. "Entomological Aspects of an Outbreak of Sleeping Sickness near Mwanza, Tanganyika Territory." *Bulletin of Entomological Research*. Vol. XIII (1923), pp. 317-370.

-----------------. "An Examination of the Tsetse Problem in North Mossurise, Portuguese East Africa." *Bulletin of Entomological Research*. Vol. XI (1921), pp. 315-385.

-----------------. "An Experiment in Control of Tsetse Flies at Shinyanga, Tanganyika Terriorty." *Bulletin of Entomological Research*. Vol. XV (1925), pp. 95-103.

Young, C. "Conservation Policies in the Royal Forests of Medieval England." *Albion*. Vol. 10, No. 2 (1978), pp. 85-103.

Newspapers

African Standard, 1903-1905 (thereafter *East African Standard*, 1905-1963).

Dar es Salaam Times, 1919-1926 (thereafter *Tanganyika Times*, 1926-1930; thereafter Tanganyika Standard, 1930-1963).

East Africa, 1924-1935 (thereafter *East Africa and Rhodesia*, 1935-1963).

Illustrated London News, 1895-1963.

Kenya Weekly News, 1928-1969.

Leader of British East Africa, 1908-1922.

The Pioneer, The British East Africa and Uganda News, 1908.

The Sunday Telegraph, (London), 1979-1980.

The Times (London), 1895-1980.

Uganda Herald, 1912-1955.

Journals

Kenya Wild Life Society. *Annual Reports.* 1956-1963.

Dissertations

Bair, H.M. "Carl Peters and German Colonialism." Ph.D., Stanford, 1968.

DeKiewiet, Marie. "History of the Imperial British East Africa Company," 1876-1895. Ph.D., University of London, 1955.

Kelly, Nora. "In Wildest Africa: The Preservation of Game in Kenya, 1895-1933." Ph.D., Simon Fraser University, 1978.

Maforo, David Dhlalangami. "Black-White Relations in Kenya Game Policy: A Case Study of the Coast Province, 1895-1963." Ph.D., Syracuse University, 1979.

Talbot, L.M. "Ecology of Western Maasailand, East Africa." Ph.D., University of California-Berkeley, 1963.

INDEX